The Science
of the Obvious

The Science of the Obvious

Education's Repetitive Search for What's Already Known

R. Barker Bausell

ROWMAN & LITTLEFIELD
Lanham • Boulder • New York • London

Published by Rowman & Littlefield
A wholly owned subsidary of The Rowman & Littlefield Publishing Group, Inc.
4501 Forbes Boulevard, Suite 200, Lanham, Maryland 20706
www.rowman.com

Unit A, Whitacre Mews, 26-34 Stannary Street, London SE11 4AB

British Library Cataloguing in Publication Information Available

Library of Congress Cataloging-in-Publication Data Available

ISBN 9781475838138 (cloth : alk. paper)
ISBN 9781475838145 (pbk. : alk. paper)
ISBN 9781475838152 (electronic)

∞™ The paper used in this publication meets the minimum requirements of American
National Standard for Information Sciences—Permanence of Paper for Printed Library
Materials, ANSI/NISO Z39.48-1992.

Printed in the United States of America

Dedicated to my grandson:
Ronan Barker Irwin

Contents

Acknowledgments

I would like to express my gratitude to Harold Murai, PhD, of the California State University, Sacramento for his helpful comments on an early draft of the manuscript. Gratitude is also extended to the many, many educational researchers from the past and present whose work influenced this book— scientists too numerous to list and many of whom would probably prefer not to be. However, Edward Thorndike, J. M. Stephens, Doug Ellson, Benjamin Bloom, David Berliner, Betty Hart, Todd Risley, and W. James Popham must be mentioned because of their contributions to the discipline of educational research itself. Finally, I would like to thank Thomas F. Koerner (vice president and publisher) and Carlie Wall (associate editor) of Rowman & Littlefield for their competent help and support in seeing this project through to completion.

Introduction

At its best, science is about discovery and explaining why things work the way they do. However, what if there was a science that did neither? A science that repeats itself year after year but nothing new is ever discovered that everyone's great grandparents didn't already know? A science into which billions of dollars are poured but nothing results but obvious findings accompanied by platitudes? A science ostensibly designed to improve schools and the instruction of society's youth but provides no guidance in how to do so?

Unfortunately, there is such a science—it is called the *science of education*, and its practitioners have basically been unwittingly perpetrating a scam for decades—most not even realizing that they are doing nothing more relevant to classroom instruction than counting classroom ceiling tiles—others either not caring, seeing no viable options, or consoling themselves with comfortable tenured careers and mid-six-figure annual salaries.

It is a discipline, like many others, where individual scientists are judged by how many repetitive papers they write and the size of the research grants they are able to garner. But unlike *any* others, this discipline is charged with improving the education of all society's children while doing nothing to reduce the socioeconomic educational disparities of large segments of that society—other than indignantly expressing rueful lamentations regarding such inequities.

All this in a discipline that produces huge numbers of PhDs without providing any actual scientific training about *what* should be investigated, only about general methods of how to conduct research devoid of any useful purpose. A science in which, four decades ago, there was a common adage that existed among educational researchers (a fraternity to which the present author belonged at that time) called the *grandmother principle*; a principle succinctly stated as:

> *You never discover anything in educational research that your grandmother didn't already know.*

While few twenty-first-century educational researchers are familiar, or would publically agree, with this ancient principle (which could now be generationally updated to the great-grandmother principle), everyone in the discipline is familiar with complaints about the irrelevancy of educational research to everyday schooling practices made by teachers and school administrators.

And the chances are that few twenty-first-century education professors could identify an actual research study that either invalidated this principle or that resulted in improved learning in one of the nation's struggling school districts. And just a few more than none have probably ever considered the implications of this truly astonishing failure, much less been forced to take up a gauntlet, such as the encapsulated implications of the following thought question:

> *If no educational research had been conducted during this century, would this have deleteriously impacted the American public schools?*

Now certainly some educational researchers have conscientiously labored over the years to disprove the grandmother principle by discovering something that will improve the education of our young, and some are still doing so. But inevitably, even the most prolific and conscientious of educational researchers never seem to succeed. And the reason for this failure to discover anything revolutionary (or simply useful) is very simple but completely counterintuitive:

> *We already know (and have known at least since the turn of the century) just about everything there is to know about classroom learning*—which is:

1. Most students will learn what they are taught if they can understand the instruction and if they attend to it.
2. The more instruction students receive, the more they will learn.
3. The more *relevant* the instruction, the more will be learned (where "relevant" is defined as *instruction that can be understood, is attended to, involves a topic that has not already been learned [or if it has, has not been forgotten], and is assessed by an appropriate test*).
4. The learning deficits exhibited by children who come from instructionally impoverished home learning environments cannot recover from these initial disparities without massive infusions of additional instruction in quantities that schools alone are presently incapable of providing.

And these four very, very *obvious* and somewhat redundant principles lead to one almost equally obvious, very succinct, law of school learning (the evidence for which has been presented in considerable detail elsewhere [Bausell 2010] and will be only briefly reviewed here). And that very succinct (far too parsimonious to the more insecure members of a profession dedicated to make the simple sound sophisticated) law is:

> *The only way to increase the amount students learn is to increase the amount of instruction they receive and/or its relevance.*

Now, of course, many of our know-it-all grandmothers (*and* even great-grandmothers) would most likely contemptuously reply to this twenty-two-word law by saying:

> *"That's obvious, everybody knows that. Get to the point."*

But alas, for better or worse, that *is* the point and it is why the science of education could just as easily be called *The Science of the Obvious*. It is also why just about everyone, other than its practitioners, ignores educational research.

If a remedy is to be found for this sad, almost comical (but certainly ironic) state of affairs, it is necessary to review the discipline's more productive past in which a number of useful (if obvious) discoveries were actually made; discoveries that now seem totally passé (many of which have been forgotten), but that may hold the key for reconstituting the science into a useful, integral part of society.

This little book therefore is designed to provide, in addition to the answer to the rather pejorative thought question just proposed, some understanding of how the science of education has descended into its current useless and repetitive state. (A companion volume, *Creating a Useful Science of Education: Society's Most Important and Challenging Task*, will then purpose genres of research [including specific studies] and infrastructural components necessary to change the discipline's current circular trajectory.) However, before any of this can be accomplished it is necessary to first consider the underlying (very restrictive) *purpose* of educational research itself.

THE PURPOSE OF EDUCATIONAL RESEARCH

Most people have no idea what educational researchers do or are even aware that there is such a thing as a *science* of education. Few care, but they *should*. It's their money that's being wasted and it is their children who are being shortchanged.

In stark contrast, almost everyone is aware of the truly astonishing progress made in the physical and life sciences, especially the everyday products and other remarkable inventions that have directly and tangentially resulted therefrom. Products such as antibiotics, vaccines, computers, hydrogen bombs, trips to the moon, the Internet, smartphones—the list alone would practically fill this book.

And to be fair, most scientists in these fields contribute (or will contribute) little or nothing to the common good but we give them a pass because as a group, a select few do. That and the fact that we can never be completely sure who will and who won't discover something of potential importance. (Alas Cassandra-like, a few of us know exactly who will do so in education— *absolutely no one.*)

The successes of the natural sciences have rubbed off on a plethora of other social and behavioral sciences (e.g., psychology, sociology, political science, economics), each with dozens of subdisciplines whose practitioners promise taxpayers and their representatives that they will learn something of societal interest (or even importance) such as how people think, behave, interact in groups, invest in the stock market, vote, and so forth.

So far, these sciences haven't made good on their promises, but they too are given a pass because they *might* discover something of passing interest. After all, knowledge for its own sake (and the pursuit thereof) is a culturally ingrained value in most affluent societies. However, an important question for education is:

> *Is the search for knowledge for its own sake a sensible (or even achievable objective) for the science of education?*

Or even:

> *Is the creation of knowledge that bestows no benefit to students or their parents a sufficient reason for this science's continued generous public support?*

Education itself is usually classified as a behavioral science because it was originally an unloved offspring of psychology. However, it occupies a relatively unique position among its behavioral (and social) peers because its original reason for existence was purely utilitarian (and remains the reason for its continued financial support as far as taxpayers and their representatives are concerned). Its purpose is *not* to simply *produce* knowledge for its own sake or even discover something interesting. After all, *what do these platitudes even mean in the context of a classroom full of students?* Counting ceiling tiles?

Instead, what all socially conscious individuals expect the purpose of educational research to be is the *improvement* of the educational process. They expect all facets of the educational community to contribute to the goal of educating society's youth as effectively as possible, partly because of the country's belief in the necessity of a populace sufficiently educated to operate the theoretically upwardly mobile capitalistic democracy our founding fathers created for us. Thus in this sense, at least, education goes to the head of the social and behavior scientific class in terms of societal *importance*.

So from these and several other perspectives, education is a very *odd* science. On one hand, it is certainly among the most *plebian* of sciences. Few activities in life are more mundane to the causal spectator than an instructor standing in front of a classroom of twenty-five or thirty students trying to teach them the algorithm for performing multidigit division. (An extremely boring activity for most of the participants of such instruction as well, but they are captives of the situation whose attendance is required by law so no one cares about them. After all, we were all students once and we were taught how to perform "long division" because once there weren't calculators on personal computers and smartphones to do it for us.)

But while there is little possibility of uncovering many tidbits of either *interesting* or *useful* knowledge within such a setting (other than occasionally realizing that many topics no longer need to be taught at all), there is *something* of crucial *importance* in need of improvement. Far too many children chronically fail to learn what is taught and some teachers perpetually fail to teach effectively.

Remedying this situation is therefore one of the prime expectations for the science of education. Not to uncover universal truths or fascinating fillers for the media's websites, but to improve learning and instruction in our schools. For the children who fail to thrive in the traditional classroom setting become adults who (along with their children and perhaps their children's children) are relegated to less-desirable jobs, less access to the best health care, and by default are denied the promise of upward economic and social mobility in our (very) theoretically casteless society.

Of course, most educational researchers would categorically oppose this plebian, utilitarian view of their science. However, if the science is viewed from the perspective of being an exclusively applied discipline that exists solely to facilitate learning and instruction, then education is surely among the most successful of sciences (and certainly at the head of the social and behavioral scientific class) because:

The underlying mechanisms necessary for optimizing learning have already been discovered.

And none of these involve never-observed, theoretical placeholders such as black matter or "God particles" because education deals with observable *behaviors*.

But What If None of This Is True?

Well, even absurd assumptions can lead to interesting implications if they are logically derived. So let's devote a few pages to see where this one takes us, akin to our acceptance of the premise of a thought experiment or a science fiction novel.

If the proposition that we know just about everything there is to know about the classroom model is accepted as a given, what is left for the profession other than to *apply* that knowledge to the education of children? In other words, shouldn't the science of education adopt the mantle of a strictly engineering discipline whose exclusive job would be the construction of *products, apparatuses, accessories, processes, or devices that facilitate learning*?

Of course, even if this implication is logically derived, it is extremely doubtful that the discipline is capable of such a metamorphosis without some sort of draconian external intervention which this little book obviously is not. Business as usual is simply too comfortable (and, for some, profitable).

However, the good or bad news (depending upon one's perspective) is that just as the pay phone that irritatingly required the correct change evolved to one accepting credit cards, which in turn gave way to digital phones (a) that we can talk to and (b) that answer many of our most immediately pressing questions—so too will these changes come to the education process—with or without any consent or participation by educational researchers.

So one of the purposes of this little book is to serve as a wakeup call to the discipline, which the present author optimistically hopes will become an actual science of education someday rather than a scientific parody. And that happens to also be the primary purpose of the originally proposed thought question regarding what the impact upon our schools *would* have been if the discipline had been completely abandoned in the not so distant past.

Now, of course, there is no mystery regarding what the reflexive answer from 99 percent of educational researchers (and aspirants to that profession) to this thought *would* be:

"Of course the educational process would have suffered grievously!"

But to extend our thought question to a thought *experiment*, let's pretend that a member of this hypothetical 99 percent majority was tasked with addressing a room full of inner-city, low-income, single parents of first-grade children to explain why the educational research funds allocated to his or her school of education shouldn't be reallocated to *their* elementary schools for the express purpose of supplying tutoring for *their* children.

Certainly, our hypothetical academic could wax eloquently regarding the importance of (and payoff resulting from) the *pursuit* of knowledge using examples from other disciplines such as physics or biology or medicine. But it is extremely doubtful that any educational examples that actually impacted *their* children's classroom instruction would be proffered, much less from the speaker's specific school of education. And if such a finding were to come to mind, it surely wouldn't transcend the grandmother principle (or would be so *obvious* that anyone with any social sensibility would be embarrassed to mention it in front of this particular audience).

So even if everything said to this point appears to border on the demented, try to suspend disbelief for a few pages while we consider just how simple the science of education actually is and later whether it is *redeemable* given a paradigmatic change. But first, let's narrow our focus a bit.

FOUR BROAD, PAINLESS, AND (AS ALWAYS) OBVIOUS DEFINITIONS

Four definitions are required by our single, succinct law of learning proposed for the discipline (hereafter referred to as our *working hypothesis*) which was:

> *The only way to increase the amount students learn is to increase the amount of instruction they receive and/or its relevance.*

This hypothesis conceptually frames the science of education as the most uncluttered and simple science possible—basically being comprised of only four components, each bearing a logical relationship to one another. What discipline could possibly be more straightforward? And for those who prefer complex and flashy diagrams, this one may be a bit disappointing:

$$\text{Curiculum} \rightarrow \text{Instruction} \rightarrow \text{Learning} \approx \text{Testing}$$

This model is not only succinct, but extremely restrictive when its components are defined and their relationships with one another delineated. The curriculum is simply what is purposefully taught (*instruction*) in order to be *learned* which is documented by *testing*.

Said another way, the curriculum is the content that someone or some group decides needs to be taught because it is believed to be important for *some* purpose (whether personal [e.g., improves students' life satisfaction] or societal (e.g., improves students' later productivity in the workplace or makes them better citizens). *Type of instruction* is a bit more broadly defined as anything that results in learning and includes:

- Being lectured to in a classroom setting;
- Taking tests and quizzes accompanied by feedback on the answers provided;
- Feedback on performance in general;

- Being tutored;
- Completing computerized/online instructional modules;
- Being presented a word, phrase, or nonsense syllable and told to memorize it;
- Completing homework;
- Engaging in self-study;
- Reading;
- Memorization;
- Being read to;
- Watching television (educational or otherwise) and engaging in other modalities of instruction or entertainment;
- Surfing the Internet;
- Listening to others (whether in class, at the dinner table, in the crib, or peer conversations);
- Being the beneficiary of direct parental teaching;
- Being corrected by parents;
- Observing and subsequently modeling parental or peer-group behaviors;
- Observing and experiencing the environment;
- Visiting institutions with instructional agendas such as a churches, museums, and science centers;
- Engaging in social media and otherwise interacting with peers;
- Texting, being texted, and otherwise engaging in certain smartphone uses; and
- Others not yet invented or known to the present author.

Learning is more narrowly conceptualized. Someday, it may be defined in terms of electrical-neurological responses in the brain, but for current educational (and educational research) purposes, it is defined as behavioral changes resulting from *instruction* and measured by *testing*. The equivalence symbol ($\approx$) in the above "diagram" is used to denote the fact that operationally *testing* defines what has been *learned* which makes the two constructs inseparable—admittedly a bit unsatisfying (similar to the sophistic scenario regarding an unobserved tree falling in a forest), but for educational *research* purposes unobserved or undocumented learning might as well be learning that never occurred.

Testing is therefore defined as instruction-induced changes on performance of written items, oral responses to questions, improvement in physical activities/tasks, or observed behaviors of some sort. (Note that while, historically, learning has been broken into original learning, retention of learning, and its transfer or application, for present purposes we'll concentrate on "originally" learning something for the first time and discuss the other two components along with their assessment later.)

But while that's "all" there is to this science, this doesn't provide much help with answering the thought question regarding what would have happened if educational research had disappeared from the planet. To answer this question, we will need to take a whirlwind tour of twelve research genres along with a very cursory tour of the Institute of Education Science's "What Works Clearinghouse."

But first, let's begin our journey by examining some *alternative* views of what the science of education is about, since most modern academics don't appear to be particularly interested in the curriculum, instruction, learning, *or* testing.

Chapter 1

Some Examples of Educational Research That Aren't

No one has any idea how many educational research studies have been published (and certainly not how many have been conducted but not published). We do know that the Education Resources Information Center (ERIC), a division of Institute of Education Science, has amassed a list (most with abstracts) of over 1.6 *million* educational documents which comprise 479,693 "research-*related*" articles published in 1,108 journals. However, these numbers undoubtedly reflect only a fraction of the total educational-research effort since many (perhaps most) research studies are never added to the ERIC database.

Hopefully no one (at least for their sake) has read more of these studies than the present author, so in this section he will simply list a few of his *least*-favorite examples. All are from the flagship research publication of the American Educational Research Association (AERA), the largest (twenty-five thousand+ paying members) and most prestigious scholarly organization ostensibly devoted exclusively to the conduct of educational research.

This publication, aptly named the *American Educational Research Journal*, and fondly referred to by researchers as AERJ, is the most cited purely educational research journal. It is also the most coveted scientific outlet for the discipline, and all its published studies are rigorously reviewed by panels of "educational research experts" (which is [*spoiler alert*] pretty much an oxymoron).

To capture the flavor of some of these studies that do not involve any known aspect of our curriculum-to-testing model, where possible the authors' descriptions (denoted by quotation marks) are taken from the study abstracts. [The bracketed text represents the present author's sometimes irreverently snarky comments.]

Example #1: *Educational Computer Use in Leisure Contexts: A Phenomenological Study of Adolescents' Experiences at Internet Cafés* (Cilesiz 2009). This study consisted of in-depth phenomenological interviews with six Turkish students who enjoy the "leisure context" of Turkish Internet cafés. ("Phenomenological" is defined by the online *Free Dictionary* as "A philosophy or method of inquiry based on the premise that reality consists of objects and events as they are perceived or understood in human consciousness and not of anything independent of human consciousness.") Those for whom this seems like a sensible (or even meaningful) educational-research topic will find the next few examples worth the price of this book.

Example #2: *Academic Discussions: An Analysis of Instructional Discourse and an Argument for an Integrative Assessment Framework* (Elizabeth et al. 2012). "The authors examine the quality of academic discussion, using existing discourse analysis frameworks designed to evaluate varying attributes of classroom discourse. To integrate the overlapping qualities of these models with researchers' descriptions of effective discussion into a single instrument, the authors propose a matrix that (1) moves from a present/absent analytic tendency to a continuum-based model and (2) captures both social and cognitive facets of quality academic discourse." [If this language is typical, surely "quality academic discourse" is another oxymoron.]

Example #3: *Power and Collaboration—Consensus/Conflict in Curriculum Leadership: Status Quo or Change?* (Ylimaki and Brunner 2011). [This one does at least mention the curriculum in its title, but for some reason the authors weren't awarded an expenses-paid trip to Stockholm despite their persuasive and erudite explanation of the importance of their research.] Again from the abstract: "This exploratory article draws on multiple theoretical lenses and empirical research to focus on collaboration-consensus/conflict and power as experienced within literacy curriculum change efforts. Conflict and collaboration processes are discussed in the literature but remain dualistic and lack the nuance of deeper understanding." [A colleague with whom the present author shared this quote suggested that it be explained in "layman's" terms, but unfortunately your author has no idea what these two investigators were talking about. Sorry.]

Example #4: *Young Children Making Sense of Racial and Ethnic Differences: A Sociocultural Approach* (Park 2011). Classroom participant observation and interviews with six focal students [ranging in age from 3 to 5] revealed children actively constructing understandings by appropriating various social tools. The children in this study enacted racial and ethnic identities, constructed theories about how differences operate, formed peer groups, and made sense of the multitude of messages they received about diversity." [Now this is impressive. Three-year-olds can do all of this? No wonder your authors' adult children aren't able to support him in his old age, forcing him to write best sellers such as this. His children had only recently learned to talk by that age, much less make "sense of the multitude of messages they received about diversity."

Example #5: *The Correlates of Tracking Policy: Opportunity Hoarding, Status Competition, or a Technical-Functional Explanation?* (Kelly and Price 2011). Perhaps fearing that they could not adequately communicate the importance of this study through its title, the authors transparently and lucidly describe their article in the abstract as follows: "In this analysis, the authors explore the relationship between the social context of high schools and school-to-school variation in tracking policies. The authors consider three explanations for the implementation of highly elaborated tracking systems: opportunity hoarding, status competition, and a technical-functional explanation." [The present author's unfamiliarity with these "explanations" is either an illustration of his intellectual limitations; the belief that a technical, discipline-specific language cannot substitute for actual scientific inquiry; or both. He did consider "opportunity hoarding" an attractive behavior and might engage in it himself if he knew how.]

Example #6: *Tailoring New Urban Teachers for Character and Activism* (Boggess 2010). "Drawing on urban regime analysis and resource dependence theory, the study asked how the reform partners defined 'teacher quality' and how the structure of their partnerships contributed to those meanings. The study produced findings indicating participants' preferences for varying types of professional dispositions considered essential to teacher quality. The study considered the implications of reform partners 'tailoring' teachers to possess specific sets of dispositions in order to fulfill ideal constructions of teacher quality and meet the instructional needs of each district." [Given the existence of discipline-specific terms employed in many of the more successful sciences, it isn't surprising that a low-status science such as education would expend considerable effort in inventing new terms and refining definitions of existing ones, such as "teacher quality." Aficionados of such linguistic conventions should be thankful for the existence of regime analysis and resource-dependence theory, without which such definitions wouldn't be possible and the above quote would have made no sense at all.]

Example #7: *Language and Literacy for a New Mainstream* (Enright 2011). "This article presents cases of three young people who represent the 'New Mainstream' of the 21st-century classroom as they engaged in a year-long research and writing project. . . . Findings suggest the need for a reframing of the notion of 'mainstream' and expanded definitions of academic language to better address the realities of New Mainstream classrooms." [This is educational research at its close-to-most-efficient form; where one needs to only talk to three people instead of the usual six to both represent the entire population of twenty-first-century students and to determine the need for better definitions of such key terms as the "new mainstream."]

Example #8: *What Is Diversity? An Inquiry into Preservice Teacher Beliefs* (Silverman 2010). "The term *diversity* seems to carry a wide array of definitions. These definitions can affect the ways teachers understand and employ the term as well as the ways in which they approach sociocultural differences in their classrooms." [You guessed it. The teachers needed more work on defining diversity. Perhaps definition construction should have been added as a fifth key educational construct in the complex diagram presented a few pages earlier?]

Example #9: *Changing Stories: Trajectories of Identification among African American Youth in a Science Outreach Apprenticeship* (Polman and Miller 2010) "This article reports on a descriptive study of youth identity as developing through 'trajectories of identification' in a science outreach apprenticeship program designed to transition urban African American youth to professional work and career aspirations. A sociocultural framework of identity development is utilized, incorporating the notions of prolepsis, negotiated identity positioning, taking on roles of agency and purpose, and working in a borderland that hybridizes culture." [Obviously, it's not just definition formation that needs to be added to important educational research topics; reading this study leads one to suspect that a key purpose of the schooling process itself may be to incorporate prolepsis through negotiated identity positioning, in order to function in the borderland that hybridizes culture—the present author's bad!].

Example #10: *The Co-Construction of Opposition in a Low-Track Mathematics Classroom* (Hand 2010). "Analysis of the classroom interaction revealed the emergence and escalation of a number of classroom practices that became oppositional. These practices were related to the nature of the mathematical activity, the framing and positioning of student participation in this activity, and multiple interpretations of student competence in and out of the classroom. The author found that classroom opposition is fostered by weak opportunities for meaningful mathematical engagement and the transformation of a polarized participation structure into an oppositional one." [*Translation:* Some of the students who were poor at math, didn't like to be taught math, and would rather be doing something else.]

SO WHY DON'T MORE PEOPLE LEARN ABOUT GROUND-BREAKING RESEARCH SUCH AS THIS?

That's a very difficult question, since more studies such as this could surely turn around poorly functioning schools and reduce the disparities in the amount children learn. And while the present author is no fan of conspiracy theories, something nefarious does seem to be going on here to hide this work from the public at large.

And with cutting-edge research such as this, why have other disciplines looked down on their educational colleagues ever since education departments have been added to universities? Don't they want learning to be improved in schools serving economically challenged and racially segregated schools? How else can this be done other than equipping a purely practice-based discipline with sound scholarship, an enviable professional language that no outsiders can decipher, and useful research findings such as these?

Obviously it is incumbent for experienced [some might unkindly say "really old"] academicians such as the present author to publicize the accomplishments of this societally crucial discipline. One cannot avoid feeling sorry for education doctoral students who encounter sneers or pejorative interrogatives (e.g., *"Really?"*) when they identify their field to their peers in other disciplines over beers or between drags.

Perhaps the following advice might be helpful to *any* educational academics who find themselves in this unenviable position (whether a student at a fraternity party *or* the Secretary of Education addressing a hostile congressional committee *or* a reform minded superintendent of schools addressing a belligerent group of low-income parents complaining that their fourth-grade children can't read). Why not simply always keep a copy of our eleventh and (almost) final example published in the *AERJ* in their pocket to whip out and proudly announce "This is the type of research I'm training to do!" *or* "This is the type of research I'm asking the House of Representatives to fund!" *or* "This is the type of research that will allow me to reform our schools and avoid a state takeover!"

And it wouldn't hurt, unless it's situationally untenable, to let these scientist-wannabes, useless politicians, or ungrateful parents know that this seminal study involved an interview of two (not three, not six) teachers. Then, just sit back and confidently exult in the resulting expressions on their previously smug, incredulous, or belligerent faces!

Example #11: *Whiteness Enacted, Whiteness Disrupted: The Complexity of Personal Congruence* (Chubbuck 2004). "This study of the enactment and disruption of Whiteness in two White secondary literacy teachers . . . demonstrated some disruption of Whiteness as well as some continued enactment of Whiteness, despite their stated intentions. The findings indicate that neither an abolition of Whiteness nor a rearticulation of Whiteness includes a sufficiently complex understanding of how disruption of Whiteness is influenced by the interplay of personal identity, the need to maintain personal congruence, and the cultural constraints of Whiteness. The author suggests that the inclusion of a psychological framework will be valuable in further exploration of the disruption of Whiteness." [So for our purposes here, perhaps we should add the development of psychological frameworks for key educational concepts such as "The Interruption of Whiteness" to our to-do lists of important educational research efforts?]

But wait! Is it possible to conduct envy-producing, funding-eliciting, mob-dispersing research with *fewer* than two interviewees?

Example #12: *Why Is Dissemination So Difficult? The Nature of Teacher Knowledge and the Spread of Curriculum Reform* (Craig 2006). "Anchored in the narrative inquiry tradition, this article examines commonly held beliefs about curriculum dissemination from the perspective of a teacher whose campus participated in a major school reform initiative. Through the presentation of a constellation of fine-grained stories revolving around the teacher's curriculum making as an art educator, the integral role that narrative played in the elucidation of her knowledge, most specifically her emerging understanding of curriculum development and dissemination, comes to light. At the same time, the underside of technical rationalism, the taken-for-granted worldview that dominates Western society and drives educational policy, is exposed and held open to scrutiny." [Now this truly *is* impressive. The entire underside of Western society's technical rationalism can be exposed from talking to one art teacher! What was Alfred Nobel thinking when he failed to designate a prize for educational research? How could anyone ignore such a science?]

DOES EDUCATIONAL RESEARCH REALLY HAVE SUCH A BAD REPUTATION?

Yes, it does, and if both the public and the profession itself didn't tend to completely ignore the entire discipline (hence never encountering some of the foibles illustrated above), educational research would possess an even worse reputation than it currently enjoys.

Because more explicitly:

1. Educational research is a completely failed discipline from several perspectives. It is noncumulative in nature, unhelpful to clinicians and policy makers, and proceeds not in a linear trajectory but in a sort of "do loop."
2. The science has no clear agenda, hence neither do most educational researchers themselves other than to publish a sufficient number of papers (or other vitae-padding pursuits) in order to attract external funding and/ or to achieve tenure.
3. The theories and paradigms that *should* guide these researchers' efforts do not because they are primarily linguistically based and profoundly bromidic in nature.
4. Education is a practice-oriented discipline dealing with instruction in useful curricula designed to produce learning as measured by testing, hence the purpose of a *science* of education is to facilitate one or more aspects

of this practice—an assumption that is most obviously either not accepted or understood by the vast majority of the discipline.

Some do understand the discipline's spectacular failings, however; perhaps rather kindly encapsulated by Professor Ellen Condliffe Lagemann's understated title of what is sadly considered *the* definitive book dealing exclusively with the history of the discipline (*An Elusive Science: The Troubling History of Education Research*, 2000). Sadly, this history is almost exclusively devoted to the funding and politics related to the discipline and not to research examples (salutary, demented, or otherwise)—a deficiency that the present book is designed to ameliorate, although it is not a history in any systematic sense.

But from an unsystematic historical perspective, let's take a quick tour over the years of the rending of garments regarding discontent with the state of educational research by some who are at least aware of the existence of this much-criticized and unloved discipline—and let's not forget *ignored* by teachers, parents, school administrators, teacher educators, the public, politicians, and other scientists.

Garment Rending Example #1: *"The Awful Reputation of Education"* (Kaestle 1993)

Written partly in response to an influential national report breathlessly advocating more funding for the Office of Educational Research and Improvement while suggesting reorganization thereof (Atkinson and Jackson 1992), the author, another specialist in the history of American education, informally interviewed thirty-three key agency officials and researchers with varying opinions regarding the etiology of educational research's unenviable reputation.

Noting that "congress created the National Institute of Education in 1972 because they believed that the research programs of the Office of Education were mediocre and useless," the author concluded that many members of congress apparently hadn't changed a great deal in the ensuing decades (believing that education research and development "doesn't pay off").

As an aside, the National Institute of Education was itself abolished in 1985 (presumably for similar reasons), with some of its functions transferred to the Office of Educational Research and Improvement, which (you guessed it) was abolished in 1992 in favor of the creation of the Institute of Education Sciences (IES), which is now part of the US Department of Education.

These occasional abolitions and inevitable rebirths extend to universities as well. The University of Chicago and Johns Hopkins University, once possessive of the most prestigious colleges of education in the country, wound up abolishing them completely. Hopkins has reinstituted theirs, first as a night school then as a full-fledged cash cow; Chicago not yet as of this writing—but it probably will eventually.

The author (Kaestle), formerly on the faculty at Harvard, University of Chicago, and Brown, attributed at least part of this discontent to everyone's familiarity with the schooling process:

> Everybody's been to fourth grade, so everybody knows what good teaching is.
>   You can't make your own ICBM or cure cancer, but you know how history should be taught and you know how kids should be disciplined. (Kaestle 1993, 27)

This leads, in his opinion, to the following reaction whenever congress is informed of an educational research finding funded by the federal government:

> You've just spent $3 million to tell me what I knew from the time I was in the fourth grade. (Kaestle 1993, 28)

Of course, this phenomenon is subsumed under the major educational research tenet that forms the title of this book (i.e., *The Grandmother Principle* and *The Science of the Obvious*, respectively for those not paying attention or who ordered the book by mistake). And $3 million wouldn't even buy first-grade-level knowledge today.

Garment Rending Example #2: *"Improving the 'Awful Reputation' of Educational Research"* (Sroufe 1997)

Apparently written only four years later as a timely response to Kaestle's complaint (which is cited in the first sentence of this article), this author suggests that the poor reputation of education research is a function of both "(1) what education research cannot do and (2) what education research does not do" (p. 27).

Among the things education research does not do, according to Sroufe, is "provide critical, trustworthy, policy-relevant information about problems of compelling interest to the education public." Picky, picky! Still, a position which very few people would have disagreed with then or now, other than perhaps now to include it under the first category, "what education research cannot do" (p. 27).

Garment Rending Example #3: *"Why Do Educational Research? Rethinking Our Roles and Identities, Our Texts and Contexts"* (Peterson 1998)

Here, a candidate for the presidency of the AERA punctuates her apparently successful campaign speech with:

Why do educational research? The public holds educational research in low esteem; policymakers increase funding for reform but not for research. Is this a "wake-up call"? (Peterson 1998, 4)

If it was, her audience must have long since gone back to sleep.

Garment Rending Example #4: *"Educational Research: The Hardest Science of All"* (Berliner 2002)

Here, yet another president of AERA weighs in, declaring that "easy-to-do science is what those in physics, chemistry, geology, and some other fields do" while educational research is (as his title suggests) "the hardest science of all" (p. 18). And lest someone think that our *parent* discipline (which has long chased the elusive goal of knowledge for its own sake) doesn't have similar insecurities (although stating them a bit more reservedly, as is that profession's style):

Garment Rending Example #5: *"The Seemingly Quixotic Pursuit of a Cumulative Psychological Science"* (Curran 2009)

The goal of any empirical science is to pursue the construction of a cumulative base of knowledge upon which the future of the science may be built. However, there is mixed evidence that the science of psychology can accurately be characterized by such a *cumulative progression* [italics added]. (Curran 2009, 77)

Unfortunately, the evidence is not mixed anymore for psychology, given the seminal work of the Open Science Collaboration (2015), a group of 270 investigators who replicated one hundred psychological studies (i.e., conducted all one hundred again under practically identical conditions) and found that (a) the effect sizes in the replicated studies were half that of the originals and (b) while 97 percent of the original studies reported statistical significance (i.e., 97 percent of these studies came out as the investigators either wanted or expected them to), only 36 percent of their replications did so. [In science this is called *publication bias*, which is primarily caused by journals' reluctance to accept any study for publication (and concomitantly investigator reluctance to submit it thereto) that doesn't report statistical significance, which is defined in terms of a finding having "only" a one in twenty chance of occurring by pure chance.]

And this, Dear Reader, is the *parent* science that so many in education look upon with undisguised envy. But this book is about education, not psychology, and fortunately no one cares enough to precisely replicate ten educational studies, much less one hundred, although there is little doubt the results would differ if they did. After all, psychology gave birth to the science of education and, if anything, its research is methodologically sounder than education's, although its studies are equally trivial.

Replicability aside, however, no one anywhere would characterize the science of education in terms of "a cumulative progression" and if any scientific discipline produces no "cumulative progression," then that discipline surely constitutes an utterly failed science. So let's explore some of the reasons nothing new or noteworthy or useful appears to ever emanate from educational research. At least nothing that would impress our grandmothers (or their mothers).

Chapter 2

Contributors to This Sad State of Affairs

To understand the failings of the science of education (and perhaps even to improve it, although that's an exceedingly ambitious goal), let's identify some of the culprits that have contributed to its current doldrums.

A REVIEW OF FIVE IMPEDIMENTS TO CREATING A MEANINGFUL SCIENCE OF EDUCATION

If we make the assumption that *perhaps* something may be slightly amiss that is preventing the existence or creation of a viable science of education, let's consider some possible culprits. Whether these accused miscreants are indeed guilty, no one knows. A more parsimonious explanation (which is always preferable) might simply involve insufficient scientific training, acculturation, motivation, and/or talent on the part of this failed discipline's practitioners (and/or *their* mentors).

But if this is the case, perhaps this is all a waste of time, so let's blame at least some of the failings of our science on the following problems (all of which have or will be touched upon):

Problem #1: *The lack of useful paradigms, frameworks, theories, or hypotheses* (depending upon linguistic preferences) *capable of predicting what will and will not increase school learning.* Consciously or unconsciously, all disciplines are guided by theories (which in turn are guided by paradigms) that inform their practitioners' choices of testable hypotheses. It has already been argued here that the learning theories, frameworks, hypotheses, and/ or paradigms typically available to guide educational research studies are characterized by being (a) primarily linguistic, (b) profoundly bromidic, (c)

11

informed by personal opinions rather than data, and/or (d) so diffuse that they are incapable of informing or generating a specific testable hypothesis.

Implications: the production of a plethora of tautological, repetitive, noncumulative, and/or noneffective instructional interventions. This book's attempt at ameliorating this most crucial of failings has already begun with the presentation of an explicit law of school learning that has been dubbed our working hypothesis.

Problem #2: *A lack of understanding of what constitutes meaningful educational research.* This deficit afflicts practicing researchers, their instructors/mentors, and consumers of the end product of the educational research process. Educational research, as conceived here, is an exclusively applied scientific discipline dedicated to inquiry designed to *improve* (which also includes increasing the relevance) one of the four components of the science itself: the *curriculum, instruction,* and *learning* as measured by *testing*.

The value-laden word "improvement" involves different types or genres of inquiry for each of these components, and the word "relevance" has a different connotation in each context. As *examples* of the latter, relevance of the curriculum deals with the ultimate utility of what is taught; relevance of instruction deals with how well it matches the curriculum and the learners acquisition of the necessary prerequisites thereof; relevance of testing (which again can't yet separate from learning) deals with the fidelity with which it matches both of the preceding; and relevance for all three also involves the degree to which all three can be understood and attended to (i.e., engaged) by the learner.

If all of this sounds a bit involved, the fault lies in its author's prose—not with the complexity of the science itself. And it will all be illustrated more concretely shortly by actual (or proposed) studies.

Now obviously, many thoughtful academics (even those who might question the relevance of studies involving "whiteness" or interviewing Turkish students in Internet cafés) may consider this conception of what a science of education *should* entail to be too restrictive. However, this exclusive practice orientation represents an ironclad assumption here as well as among the founders of the discipline and just about everyone else outside of academic education.

Another supposition made here that would also meet with catcalls and flying fruit from a live academic audience (which is why the present author doesn't give talks, aside from the fact he's never asked to) is the irritating contention that just about everything there is to know about instruction and learning has already been investigated. Now utterances such as this have probably been made in almost every science at some point or another, but this one may actually be true given this science's restrictive scope. No one knows, of course, and it may be completely wrong here.

However, educational researchers don't appear to realize that performing repetitions of (or small variations on) past work will not result in any meaningful advance in *any* science—just as craniologists (those intrepid early intelligence testers) never seemed to realize that a more precise method (or an ever-so-minute variant) of measuring people's heads would reveal the origins of intelligence and, more importantly, serve as a marker for those who had it and those who did not.

One also can't help but wonder how many educational researchers are aware of the sheer size of the database of past educational research involving *learning*, an embarrassment of riches (or simply an embarrassment) that precludes anyone without a clinical diagnosis of OCD from achieving anything close to a comprehensive grasp of what has already been investigated. Perhaps the most dramatic illustration of the size of this database is a compilation (and intrepid if vain attempt at summarization) of 816 educational meta-analyses involving student achievement as the outcome variable involving 52,649 individual studies and a total of 83,033,433 participants (although the author [Hattie 2009] suggests that this latter number might be as high as *236 million*).

And while there is unquestionably considerable redundancy here with respect to studies, participants, and the meta-analyses themselves, this is part of the point. Especially since these 816 meta-analyses (now grown to over a thousand) only involve topics in which enough studies have been conducted to merit such a synthesis (on average each meta-analysis in the 2009 effort contained around sixty-five studies).

Implication: So again, in a logical system even if a set of assumptions (or postulates) appear to be wrong-headed and not reflective of someone's world view, the logical implications flowing therefrom can be rather interesting and even valid. So let's see where the proposition that educational research is an exclusively applied discipline takes us:

1. Since it follows from this that the discipline's practitioners do not have the luxury of generating knowledge for knowledge's sake, the only subject matter appropriate for an educational research study involves improving some aspect of the educational process, which in turn involves improving some aspect of instruction, the curriculum guiding that instruction, and/ or the assessment of *learning* (which also includes *application/transfer or retention* thereof).
2. Since the improvement of the educational process involves such a limited number of components, the conduct of such a science would become much more focused than it is presently or ever has been in the past. Few, if any, scientific disciplines, can so explicitly delineate either their subject matters or their agendas.

3. And finally, individuals who pursue alternative lines of "research," such as the twelve mentioned in chapter 1, should formally visualize themselves in one of the earlier scenarios in which they are standing in front of a congressional hearing making a case for their continued employment for the next thirty years based upon said research. And then consider what the outcome would be. Or alternately, since we all look down on legislators, to change the locale of their testimony and pretend they are trying to convince an impoverished inner-city school board (under attack from all sides due to their students' abysmal test scores) to fund their salaries for the next thirty *days*. What do they think the outcome of that presentation would be? Perhaps something tossed worse than overripe fruit.

Problem #3: *The excessive variability between and within educational settings coupled with the excessive number of confounding variables accompanying the educational process.* Students differ within classrooms (especially those involving homogeneous placement), between classrooms (especially across schools serving different families from different socioeconomic levels [primarily income and parental-educational histories]), and everywhere with respect to grade level and age (i.e., from five years of age in kindergarten to seventeen to eighteen years of age in twelfth grade).

Added to the problem, large teacher differences exist with respect to (a) the amount of instruction they deliver, (b) their fidelity to the prescribed curriculum, and (c) their tolerance for (or ability to prevent) disruptive behavior. And as if that weren't enough, the curriculum is composed of diverse academic subjects within each grade level, each of which is segmented into multiple topics.

Implications: The reduction of this variability with respect to the mastery of the curriculum should be the primary goal of the science of education. However, some degree of individual differences in students' response to instruction will always be with us, so educational studies that do not adequately control for individual student/teacher differences (as well as a plethora of procedural controls) are almost surely doomed to failure.

Equally troublesome, *most educational experiments differ from one another by employing differing experimental environments, students with differing backgrounds, teachers with differing agendas, different curricula and therefore different tests—all of which are capable of producing different results from otherwise similarly designed studies.* So perhaps Berliner was correct, perhaps education is "the hardest science," at least from the perspective of discovering universal truth and knowledge. But that should never have been its purpose anyway.

Problem #4: *The understandable inferiority complex of the discipline's membership and their low status within academia.* This manifests itself for some through posturing like the males of certain bird species, inventing weird language conventions for commonplace concepts in order to sound like "real" scientists, and embracing other academic behaviors such as conducting meaningless studies and publishing for no other reason than to add as many pages to their vitae as possible.

Implications: There are none, except to realize that much of academia as a whole is comprised of a shell game peopled with insecure, posturing individuals, some of whom are bright enough to realize that they have contributed little to their science and nothing to the common good.

Few are perceptive (or foolish) enough, however, to question the societal usefulness of their entire *disciplines*. But there are, in fact, too many unnecessary, worthless disciplines and far too many unqualified individuals conducting worthless research in all disciplines. This is especially and dramatically true for just about *all* of the social and behavioral sciences.

However, on the bright side, no scientific discipline (with the possible exception of medicine) is potentially more important to society than education, and (perhaps not coincidentally) *none* is more rightfully insecure because of its failures. So while it may be necessary for educational scientists to engage in some of the inane behaviors required of all academics, if *any* are able to make an actually meaningful contribution to their science then their foolishness is easily forgivable.

Problem #5: *A systemic, largely unrecognized virus implanted by education's parent discipline of psychology and its early intelligence test developers*—a more in-depth discussion of which will be presented in chapter 4.

Implications: This may be the most serious of the five problems from the perspective of creating a meaningful science of education and perhaps should have been listed as Problem #1. However, since its remediation will consider a considerable amount of specific research, the proposed work and their explication will be saved for later.

And next up . . .

Now that the systemic problems with our science have been delineated, the next step is to go through the science—research genre by research genre—in an effort to identify those that have produced potential useful (if obvious) findings, those we no longer need, and perhaps those that *might* be useful in the creation of a meaningful science of education given a bit of insight and the necessary infrastructure.

Chapter 3

Four Once-Useful Influential Research Genres That We Probably No Longer Need

The four genres discussed in this chapter have been around for decades (one for over a century), but that doesn't imply the same fields need to plowed over and over again. Nevertheless, because of their historic import, they need to be at least considered along with a few noteworthy examples of all but the oldest—which is definitely a bit long of tooth and well past its prime.

GENRE #1: CLASSIC LEARNING RESEARCH

The work of Edward Thorndike (born in 1874) constitutes a logical beginning point for the empirically based science of education, although he took pains to identify his field as psychology, *not* education. Nevertheless, Thorndike right-fully deserves his preeminent historical place in both disciplines for several lines of work; the most relevant to us (or at least to our working hypothesis) probably involved his laboratory work with animals. He was wont to place these animals (often cats) in "puzzle boxes," comprised of mazes, in order see how long it took them to learn how to escape under varying conditions.

Based upon these and other work, he developed several learning principles, the three most relevant to educational research being:

1. "The law of effect," which basically stated that behaviors positively rein-forced are more likely to occur again as compared to those not reinforced;
2. "The law of exercise," which posited that learning would increase with practice, and is basically a function of *time on task or instructional time*; and
3. The generalization that the extent to which transfer of learning occurs is a function of the degree to which two tasks share a common (or almost

identical) element. If tasks are not very proximally linked and contain common elements, Thorndike predicted that no transfer will occur (hence learning Latin won't "train the brain" to learn other unrelated topics more quickly).

What is perhaps most remarkable about his work is how little we've learned since the publication of his *Animal Intelligence* in 1911 where the above principles were enunciated. But there has been some progress regarding the effects of the purposeful presentation of stimuli (instruction) in order to produce specific responses (learning) thereto, so let's move on from animal to human learning

A little later in the twentieth century, more and more investigators interested in learning began studying humans under carefully controlled conditions. Even if Thorndike was correct and people learn the same way as animals do, we can be taught a considerably expanded and very different curriculum as compared to the latter. And let's face it, we are easier to test.

Despite these advantages, however, certain additional challenges existed for this line of inquiry with human participants. Most notably the need to control such factors as (a) the possibility that the proffered instruction included topics the research participants had already learned and (b) the need to take individual teacher and participant differences into account.

Consequently, in what became to be referred to as *paired associate (or sometimes serial) learning trials*, investigators often employed nonsense syllables presented under rigidly standardized conditions. Experimental participants were taught, via repeated presentations—often involving a slide projector (for those under the age of fifty: a primitive precursor to PowerPoint or its equivalent) to learn these syllables (or sometimes words). To avoid as much error as possible in inferring that learning had occurred (and to measure it as precisely as humanly possible), testing often involved presenting the syllables, words, or whatever via exactly the same medium through which they were learned.

A huge number of carefully controlled experiments employed some variant of these methods was conducted and a good deal was discovered about the learning process: perhaps not earthshaking discoveries (many of which Thorndike had already made), but solid meat-and-potatoes findings nevertheless. Most elementally, three primary types of learning were inferred and defined by these studies:

1. *Original learning*, which is identical to what we mean when we refer to "school learning," although hopefully, the latter's curriculum is a bit more meaningful than nonsense syllables—Paul Simon's lyrics about what he learned in high school notwithstanding.

2. *Retention of learning*, which refers to how long what was learned is remembered, or to the circumstances influencing the amount and rate of forgetting.
3. *Transfer of learning*, which in classic learning theory refers to the fact that previous learning can sometimes facilitate (and sometimes even impede) subsequent learning.

And, if you think about it, these three processes pretty much reflect what we expect students to take from the schooling process:

1. Learning what is taught (which is the primary purpose of schooling);
2. Retaining it (because if we don't remember what we've learned, we have to learn it all over again—although it is learned faster the second time and may even facilitate online searching); and
3. Transfer, which includes learning related topics (which is facilitated by previous learning) and application of learning (which may be the most important educational outcome) and is a huge leap from both Thorndike's and the classic learning researchers' work. It is also one which we currently know little or almost nothing about—at least from the perspective of the subsequent *creation* of original knowledge or products.

In a nutshell, some of the findings emanating from this genre of research most relevant to classroom instruction and student learning were:

The more times a paired-associate task was repeated (which were called "learning trials," and we'll call "instructional time" here), the more learning occurred. This was by far the strongest and most consistent relationship this line of investigation ever uncovered. It was also completely consistent with Thorndike's animal trials: the more *relevant* time on task provided (or the more practice sessions afforded to running in a maze, or the more presentations of the stimuli), the more learning occurs.

(The adjective *relevant* is emphasized here because what was taught was typically exactly what was tested. Or said another way, the test perfectly matched the instruction and the instruction perfectly matched the curriculum.) This finding was so pervasive, in fact, that some researchers (Bugelski 1962; Cooper and Pantle 1967) embraced a "total-time hypothesis," which basically postulated that, within reasonable limits, the same amount would be learned in a given amount of time, regardless of the number of trials presented within that time period. (They also posited that the additional time required of distributed practice [i.e., trials in which rest periods were allowed] might explain its superiority over massed practice.)

Some forgetting of what was learned always occurred, but the more time on task (or the more presentations of the stimuli), the longer the association (or learning) was retained (remembered). Retention was also improved by (a) increasing the meaningfulness of the instructional content (which in paired-associate trials could involve moving away from nonsense syllables to employing actual words or syllables therein) and/or (b) continuing to present the stimuli even after they were originally learned (which was called *overlearning*). Of course this also reduces to time on task (or increased instructional time).

Applying what is learned (or in some applications referred to as "learning to learn") proved to be a much more tenuous affair. This can occur as an outcome of instruction (as always, broadly defined), but under rather restrictive, specialized conditions.

For example, transfer was (a) sometimes facilitated by overlearning, (b) more likely to occur when the training conditions were most similar to the ultimate testing conditions (which in schooling terms can be reflected by practices such as teaching to the test or teaching test-taking skills), and (c) apparently occurred only when the original learning task possessed certain components in common with the transfer task (an example in schooling practice would be teaching a child the sounds represented by a vowel to facilitate the subsequent learning of words containing that vowel).

Classic learning research wasn't really equipped to address such behaviors as creativity or applying knowledge to novel applications, and we still have difficulty with the concept itself—splitting its positive aspect into various categories (e.g., near, far, proximal, distal, vertical, horizontal ad nauseam).

While all of this may seem a bit off topic as far as schooling practice is concerned, *learning is learning* and, overall, classic learning research is quite supportive of our working hypothesis (not coincidentally since the latter was partially built upon the former). Also, at the end of the day, this line of inquiry shares something in common with educational research: most of its results were patently obvious and never transcended the grandmother principle. And maybe, just maybe, that's a good thing for the science of education because perhaps the very simplicity of the discipline can facilitate its future development. Or if this *doesn't* occur, perhaps the discipline's blatant obviousness will encourage the reallocation of its research funds to more sensible pursuits.

Implications for future research: There aren't any for education that the present author can ascertain, although some academic psychologists with an interest in human learning continue to conduct these studies. But why not, academics have to publish something.

To be fair, however, the genre employed some methodological procedures that deserved preserving and that were in fact adopted as good educational research practices:

1. Randomly assigning Subjects (Ss) to conditions (or conditions to Ss in repeated measures designs).
2. Ensuring that the instructional content (i.e., the curriculum) between conditions is as identical as possible.

3. Ensuring that the learning assessments matches the instructional content of all experimental conditions and are administered under the same (or very similar) conditions in which the instruction was administered.
4. Conducting experiments within carefully controlled environments rather than the madhouse that often characterizes the traditional classroom setting.
5. Delivering instruction individually, hence mimicking the tutoring paradigm.

GENRE #2: SECONDARY ANALYSES OF TEST SCORES

Here is another type of research we definitely don't need any more of without some dramatic alterations, although one of its earliest examples was probably the most influential study in the history of educational research so it has to be mentioned. Officially titled the "Equality of Educational Opportunity," but soon thereafter simply referred to as the "Coleman Report," this was the largest educational study of its kind (or perhaps of any kind) up to that point in time (Coleman et al. 1966).

The study was originally funded by the US Department of Education to investigate inequities in public education, but its primary impact on educational research (besides giving a steroidal impetus to its genre by inspiring *thousands* of other repetitive analyses of test score databases) was the basic conclusion definitively demonstrating that:

The most powerful determinants of success in school lies in what children bring to the schooling process rather than what happens to them once they get there.

Interestingly, this was hardly a new conclusion, as witnessed by John Kemp's dictum in 1955

To estimate the general academic performance that will occur in a given school, ask first about the general intellectual level of the children and the social and economic background of the parents. . . . *This information will account for almost sixty percent of all the differences that will be found from school to school."* (Kemp 1955, 50)

Both study findings (the Coleman report being by far the more influential) have been repeated many times thereafter, most notably by Benjamin Bloom (1976), who found that standardized tests administered to children as early as age three are strongly predictive of test scores obtained throughout their schooling experience.

Before presenting some modern examples of this genre, a conceit here referred to as *education urban legends* will be introduced. These can be defined as popularly held, completely fallacious professional educational beliefs that have significantly impeded the science's progress. The first two therefore are:

> Education Urban Legend #1: *Correlation equals causality (or if you control enough variables using sophisticated-sounding statistical procedures, you can determine the etiology of anything)*. It's not clear who we can blame this one on other than statisticians (although at least they call the approach causal *modeling*) or economists (who never deal with actual causation and most of whom know very little or nothing about education), but if we ever find out who the responsible really are they should be severely punished.

> Education Urban Legend #2: *Teacher effectiveness is the strongest determinant of student learning*. Wrong again. Individual differences among children that manifest themselves long before they ever step through the schoolhouse door are the strongest predictors of individual differences *after* they do so. Administer children a battery of tests the day before they attend school and the results will predict standardized achievement tests every year thereafter, high-school grades, high-school completion, SAT scores, college attendance, and just about every other academic variable imaginable.

Both of these two misconceptions are prevalent, but more space must be devoted to the latter than it would otherwise merit due to the fact that it informed one of the most influential educational policy issues of the twenty-first century: *value-added teacher evaluation*, which, its proponents proclaimed, could exponentially increase student learning in the public schools. And if this claim proved to be valid, our original thought question would be answered in the *affirmative*—thereby perhaps making this book (and its companion volume) completely unnecessary and freed the present author to spend more time with *his* companion: Jack Daniels.

The conceptual basis of teacher effects upon learning: When the present author entered graduate school a few eons ago, there had been relatively little empirical research conducted upon the consistency of teacher effects on student achievement. The only review of this work available at the time was completed by Barak Rosenshine (1970), who found only five (poorly controlled) studies assessing the stability of long-term teacher effects upon student achievement. Rosenshine's conclusion in that bygone era was:

> The current long-term studies show that one cannot use the residual achievement gain scores [i.e., subtracting beginning-of-year from end-of-year test scores] in one year to predict the gain scores in a successive year with any confidence. (Rosenshine, 1970, 661)

But that was almost half a century ago. What about now? After all, in the ensuing decades, schooling databases have proliferated, analytic techniques have grown more sophisticated, and a considerable amount of effort has been expended examining the relationship between teachers' professional characteristics (e.g., teacher knowledge, certification, experience, and training) and student achievement. Unfortunately, the results have been somewhat equivocal (and unimpressive)—partly perhaps because of a built-in confound involving the fact that schools serving inner-city, impoverished neighborhoods tend to be staffed by less-credentialed, less-experienced teachers (Hill, Rowan, and Ball 2005).

Studies such as these are typically conducted via secondary analyses of large databases including hundreds or even thousands of teachers employed in myriad schools populated by children from diverse socioeconomic backgrounds. Attempts at controlling individual differences in students' receipt of prior and current instruction due to their home environments are customarily made by statistically controlling for gross demographic factors such as (a) percentage of minority students in the teachers' schools (or classroom); (b) percentage of students eligible for free or reduced-price lunches; and/or (c) socioeconomic status (SES) (all of which are interrelated).

Thus, if teacher experience is the variable of interest, a large regression type of analysis is usually conducted in which as many covariates as possible (i.e., variables other than teacher experience [e.g., a–c above] expected to be related to student test scores) are entered into the equation as "control variables." Following this, if the resulting correlation between teacher experience (defined in terms of number of years in teaching, first-year teachers vs. all others, and so forth) and student test scores are statistically significant, then success is declared and teacher experience is shown to be a positive *determinant* of student learning.

The problems with this approach are legion, including the facts that:

1. The available databases inevitably contain a considerable amount of error, ranging from miscoded covariates to the surprisingly frequent incorrect matching of students with teachers;
2. Missing test-score data, ranging from absenteeism to student movement from school to school or transfers in and out of the school districts altogether;
3. The grossness of the covariates normally available for such analyses (e.g., SES, unquestionably related to test scores, is often assessed via a single item which is obviously absurd (see Jeynes [2002] for a thorough description of the difficulties in employing this variable);

4. The possibility that in some schools, students are consistently assigned
   to teachers based upon these students' previous test scores (perhaps, for
   example, due to parental requests or the teachers' reputation for dealing
   with certainly types of students); and perhaps most importantly of all,
5. The test scores themselves are influenced by many factors outside the
   teacher's control, including the fact that they may not be well matched
   with the curriculum being taught in an individual school, not to mention
   always being confounded with instruction received in the home environment during the school year.

However, some still argue that *if* the "control" variables are sufficiently
precise and *if* all influences upon student test scores other than teacher effects
are "subtracted out" of students' test scores and *then* teacher effects remain
correlated with student performance, what else could this be due to but *teachers*? Ignoring the fact that our control variables are far from being sufficiently
precise and we don't have measures of all of the variables that influence
student test scores, one chink in this impressive line of reasoning remains. It
is an elemental logical issue related to teacher effects that ironically Barak
Rosenshine and the authors of the studies he reviewed recognized so many
decades ago as reflected in their primary research question:

> *Regardless of whether are not teacher effects predict student performance, are
> these effects sufficiently consistent over time to have any practical importance?*

If such effects aren't consistent, then so what if an analysis of student
test score results in one specific year can be attributed to individual teacher
influences if said teacher doesn't perform consistently year after year? Said
another way: What if students taught by teacher "A" learn less than those
taught by teacher "B" one year but teacher A's students learn as much or
more than those of teacher B the next year? If this happens, what is the practical importance of such a finding?

On one level, we might predict that teacher effects probably aren't
extremely consistent based upon our working hypothesis, our first two education urban legends, and the problems with these analyses just enumerated.
But, just because something is difficult to research definitely doesn't mean
we shouldn't try to do so.

Enter the value-added teacher evaluation proponents, Stage Left: But first,
a subsidiary educational research principle which is an implication of the
grandmother principle:

> *When a new or surprising finding or position surfaces in educational research,
> it probably isn't new and if it is surprising, it probably isn't real.*

While the repetitive nature of our discipline has been lamented, it also has an exceedingly brief memory span, which is perhaps due to the size of the research database coupled with its practitioners' disinterest therein.

Interestingly, some of these repetitions actually reach the short-term status of fads that briefly catch the interest of the public, politicians (including in the present case, a president), billionaires (in this case, Bill Gates), policy "experts" (usually an oxymoron with respect to education), and even renowned economists (e.g., Eric Hanushek of Stanford University and the Hoover Institute, who assured the country [2011] that adopting value-added teacher-evaluation measures to identify and then replace the very poorest-performing teachers with *average* teachers) could generate 100 trillion dollars (not a typo) for the national economy.

Hanushek's astonishing projection aside, the advocates for hiring and firing teachers based upon their students' test scores have ignored the prerequisite question of interest regarding whether or not teacher effects are consistent from year to year. Or more precisely, since there is always a degree of inconsistency in performance due to measurement and sampling error, the key question from an educational policy perspective is the same as posed by the five authors reviewed by Barak Rosenshine a half-century ago:

How consistent/inconsistent are value-added teacher effects over time?

Fortunately, we know the answer to this question based upon one of the largest analyses of its kind which was, ironically, conducted by one of the earliest and most unabashed advocates of the process, William Sanders.

An Example of an Analysis to Determine the Consistency of Teacher Performance as Defined by Test Scores (Conducted by the Procedure's Primary Advocate)

The Performance of Highly Effective Teachers in Different School Environments

Sanders, Wright, and Langevin (2009)

These authors compared 4,906 teachers who remained in the same school district three years in a row and who were then categorized for analytic purposes as producing below-average, average, and above-average effects (using the first author's proprietary value-added approach). The following table is based upon a reconfiguration of the results presented in that article (note that Year 2 data were not available for this analysis):

Table 3.1   The "Value-Added" Consistency of Teacher Performance

Teacher Performance	Below Average (Year 3)	Average (Year 3)	Above Average (Year 3)	Total of Year 1 Value-Added Categories
Below Average (Year 1)	43%	45%	12%	941 (100%)
Average (Year 1)	21%	59%	21%	3,712 (100%)
Above Average (Year 1)	11%	44%	45%	1,253 (100%)

Altogether, there were 941 teachers who were considered below average the first year, and less than half of these same teachers (404, or 43 percent) were judged to be below average two years later based upon Sanders's much-promoted statistical manipulations. Perhaps even more remarkably, 111 (or 12 percent of the original 941) of these supposed below-average teachers (who Hanushek tacitly suggests should have been fired) were actually judged to be above average in the third year, while 45 percent moved up to the average category.

Of the 1,253 teachers judged to be above average the first year, 136 (or 11 percent) were actually below average the third year and 44 percent had regressed to the middle category. This left only 45 percent of original "high-performing" teachers in the above-average category both years.

Now consider what would have happened if the below-average teachers had all been dismissed based upon their first-year performances and replaced, as is often advocated by policy wonks. In 57 percent of these cases, the schools in question would have lost a teacher who would have performed at an average or above-average level two years later. So it is extremely doubtful that Hanushek's strategy would have generated $15 to the national economy, much less $100,000,000,000,000.

But back to the Sanders et al. analysis. If the high-performing teachers had been rewarded monetarily (which is a strategy actually implemented by several large districts) based upon their first-year performance, in over half of the cases (55 percent), the schools would have wasted their money, because these "high performers" were destined to regress back into mediocrity (or worse). The bottom line here is that only in the case of average teachers did the value-added predictive scheme produce a consistency rate of over 50 percent (actually 59 percent). For below-average and above-average teachers, the consistency of the technique was only 43 percent and 45 percent, respectively.

This level of inconsistency is much too high to base important policy decisions upon and it is too high to have any true practical implications for improving public-school education. (Another large-scale study [Aaronson, Barrow, and Sanders 2007], using citywide Chicago high-school ninth-grade math scores, produced even poorer consistency across a shorter time span.)

The bottom line here is not that there aren't such things as differential teacher effects upon student learning. We even know the most probable etiology of these effects (i.e., the differential amount of instruction some teachers deliver as opposed to others as will be illustrated shortly).

The results of value-added research *overestimate* teacher effects due to our inability to statistically control what may be the primary causative factors of student achievement in the schools (the instruction delivered or not delivered in the home environment prior to the analysis and which goes on continuously throughout the schooling experience). This huge increment of instruction is unmeasured, hence much of it gets lumped into classroom/teacher effects. But whether underestimated or overestimated, we know at least one variable that could result based upon our working hypothesis (and has been observed to result as will be illustrated shortly) in differential teacher effects upon learning—*increasing relevant instructional time.*

But believe it or not, there is a large cadre of people out there (policy makers included and all faithful adherents to our first Education Urban Legend) that cares nothing about the etiology of an effect but only the results of imperfect analyses based upon *very* imperfect standardized test databases. (One reason for this popularity is that it is so much easier to analyze electronically available data than to collect it oneself.)

Adherents to this genre of "research" appear to believe that if the statistical approaches are sophisticated enough, everything can be statistically controlled, including both confounding and causal factors—thereby making them irrelevant. The following example is tendered for the benefit of those individuals, although none of them would read a book such as this (even if there were any books such as this).

An Example of Temporally Backward "Causation" in Value-Added Teacher Evaluations Based Upon the Analysis of Large Commercial Achievement Test Databases (Or When Does the Future Influence the Past?)

Teacher Quality in Educational Production: Tracking, Decay, and Student Achievement

Jesse Rothstein (2010)

One potential problem with predictions based upon correlational data is temporal (i.e., the possibility that the inferred causal relationship emanating from analyses of existing databases runs backward in time rather than forward, since the data themselves are all retrospective). This assumption is seldom tested, but an economist named Jesse Rothstein (2010) conducted such a test on teacher value-added data.

In what began as a typical value-added analysis of a large database, Rothstein found that indeed, the performance of fifth-grade teachers' performance based upon their students' test scores (which, like all value-added analyses, is calculated by determining the difference between students' predicted end-of-year test scores for the year of interest using the same students' test scores obtained in previous years when they were taught by different teachers). This predicted end-of-year score for each student (in this case fifth grade) is then "subtracted" from their actual end-of-year test scores and the difference (averaged across all the students in a given teacher's classroom) constitutes the "value-added" by that teacher (if the number is positive, the teacher did a good job; if negative, he or she didn't). The actual computation is a bit more complicated, but this is the crux of the value-added approach.

But Rothstein didn't end his analysis after finding that the fifth-grade teachers' "performance" could indeed be predicted reasonably well by their students' test scores in fourth grade. He already knew value-added teacher evaluations "worked." What he found was that when the predictive scheme was completely reversed (i.e., when the fifth-grade performance of these students was used to compute their fourth-grade teachers' value-added performance), similar results accrued.

In other words, the fourth-grade teachers' performance (computed by subtracting their students' actually obtained fourth-grade scores and their predicted fourth-grade scores based upon their future fifth-grade test scores— which of course was obtained from different teachers) was very nicely predicted by their students' future performance. Said another way, the future caused the past.

Now, obviously, there is something very, very amiss here since causation can only move forward in time, not backward. Fifth-grade teacher performance shouldn't be able to influence fourth-grade teacher performance.

Rothstein interpreted his results as indicating that there was something quite purposeful and consistent about the way students were assigned to teachers at the beginning of the year. While he may be correct, a more parsimonious explanation involves the presence of a long-known but unmeasured determinant of learning. An unmeasured determinant of learning in this and other value-added analyses as well as all analyses based upon test score databases. A determinant whose effects extend back much further in time and persist even further into the future, and (since it isn't measured) gets "lumped" into teacher effects.

Any guesses as to what that might be? Perhaps the amount of home-based instruction delivered prior to and during the schooling process? Of course, there are other such unmeasured significant events such as parental divorces or illnesses or idiosyncratic maturation that may unpredictably occur only once in a child's life, but let's not continue to beat this now-deceased horse. (For those interested, also see Amrein-Beardsley [2008] as well as

Amrein-Beardsley and Collins [2012] for interesting methodological critiques of the value-added approach from a quite different perspective.)

Implications: As of this writing, the value-added teacher evaluation fad seems to have begun to fade, although it captured the public imagination and influenced policy more than most of its predecessors. Perhaps Jim Popham, the "father" of performance-based teacher evaluation's take on the subject sums the issue up best of all:

> There is an old saying that "data gathered with a rake should not be analyzed with a microscope." I think that in Tennessee [the site and data source of Sanders's original work] the rake-collected data are being analyzed with a *mystery* microscope. (Popham 1997, 270)

Of course, Sanders's style was a bit more enthusiastic discussing one of his findings (Sanders and Rivers 1996), to which Popham referred:

> The range of approximately 50 percentile points in student mathematics achievement in this study is awesome!!!! [His exclamation marks, not the present author's.]

So perhaps value-added teacher-evaluation advocates (and educational researchers in general) would be better served by observing the language conventions of some actual scientists in other fields, such as Watson and Crick (1953)—certainly not individuals with a propensity to hide their lights under a basket—who began a paper detailing the most heralded biological discovery of the twentieth century with:

> We wish to suggest a structure for the salt of deoxyribose nucleic acid (D.N.A.). This structure has novel features which are of considerable biological interest. (Watson and Crick 1953, 737)

While fads (by definition) tend to run their course relatively quickly, let's move on to other genres, some of the examples of which will illustrate the actual etiology of those teacher and effects that do actually exist independent of student differences.

GENRE #3: PRESCHOOL OR EXTRA-SCHOOL DESCRIPTIVE/ CORRELATIONAL EDUCATIONAL STUDIES

This is also a well-worn research arena like our first two genres but potentially far more important and certainly more relevant to present-day issues. Most of the work done in this area is correlational in nature and identifies the same correlates of lower test scores as the first two genres (i.e., lower SES, ethnicity [Asian and Caucasian families versus black and Hispanic families], lower parental educational attainment, poverty, single-mother households, children born to very young mothers, and so forth).

However, studies belonging to this genre have drilled down further than the previous category and have shown that it is the amount of instruction (broadly defined) administered in the home and family environment that is the variable most predictive of future school success. These studies have found that students do far better in school who are the beneficiaries of a home-learning environment characterized by:

1. Plentiful reading material (Senechal and LeFevre 2002),
2. Policies restricting the type and amount of television (amount of time watching educational programs has been shown to be positively related to achievement while the amount of escapist programming is negatively related [Ennemoser and Schneider 2007]), and
3. Parents who read to their children when they were young (Bus, van Ijzendoorn, and Pellegrini 1995).

Similarly, children who are actively taught the alphabet, the sounds letters make, words, numbers, number concepts, and even how to read prior to attending school obviously do better in school than children who are not so taught (see Adams [1994] for a review). Surely all of this would have been obvious to at least one great-grandmother, since one of the present author's children's great-grandmothers taught her daughter to read very early in life and, after becoming a teacher, the daughter did the same for her son.

In general, one of the primary contributions of these studies may well be their identification of the etiology of Genre #1's primary finding that the most important differentiator of individual differences in student achievement is what children bring to the schooling process rather than what occurs therein. Of course, a lot of time and energy could have been saved if we had asked our grandmothers (or great-grandmothers) what they thought was the causative factor here, but that's not science so no one asked. Besides, some would probably simply answer "their upbringing" or something equally vague.

So the specific causative factor responsible for individual differences in school achievement is *the increased instructional time (broadly defined) that some children receive both before and after they enter school.* And the positive relationship between test scores and SES is simply due to the fact that SES (of which parental education is a component) is itself strongly related to the amount of increased instruction parents provide their students outside the classroom.

From a research perspective, preschool home instruction has been the subject of most investigation, but the instruction parents administer after their children's admittance to school should not be underestimated. It encompasses

(a) tutoring (administered by parents and/or by hired professionals), (b) helping with homework, (c) ensuring that homework is completed, (d) discussing what goes on at school with children (in order to ascertaining what they are having difficulty learning as well as communicating the importance of learning itself), and so forth.

Other parental behaviors that may increase school learning (although there is not sufficiently definitive evidence for these or their relationship to SES) include (a) keeping lines of communication open with children's teachers to identify any changes in engagement or behavior (as well as making expectations clear with respect to both their children and the teachers themselves), (b) ensuring that children receive sufficient sleep, and (c) adhering to a sensible diet.

There happens to be another study, however, that if not the most important educational study ever conducted is certainly in the top three or four. Its seminal relevance to the science *and* our working hypothesis resides in differences in the sheer *amount* of instruction provided in some homes as opposed to others.

And since this study was conducted a quarter of a century ago and few, if any, twenty-first-century graduate students, practicing researchers, or members of the public have read the book that describes this landmark study, it will be abstracted here in a bit more depth than were the previous examples:

A Quintessentially Important Example of an Exemplary Preschool Observational Study

Meaningful Differences in the Everyday Experience of Young American Children

Betty Hart and Todd R. Risley (1995)

The authors frame the rationale for their study as follows:

> Virtually all children begin to acquire a vocabulary of words in the second year of life, usually soon after the first birthday. This means that a child's home and family provide the circumstances for the emergence of language and word learning. (Hart and Risley 1995, xiii)

They then proceed to describe one of the most impressive and labor-intensive studies in the history of education in which the amount of time that parents talked to their children (and the quality of that linguistic interaction) was meticulously observed for one hour per month for two and a half years beginning when the child was approximately one year old. (The investigators estimated that at least eight hours were needed to transcribe each one-hour observational period, they were unable to take a vacation for three years, and they were forced to wait six years before their data were completely analyzed.)

Dividing the forty-two families into "professional," "working-class," and "welfare" socioeconomic classifications, the investigators estimated that in an average year, the total parental communication to professional-class children was a mind-boggling eleven million words, as compared to six million for the working-class families, and three million for the welfare families. (No, this is not a typo: children from professional families were the beneficiaries of five million more words than working-class families, and eight million more than welfare parents per year.)

The complexity of this speech (e.g., vocabulary, grammar) and the proportion of encouraging phrases (e.g., "You're so smart!") versus negative tones/ imperatives (e.g., "Don't do that!") varied similarly in the expected direction, but the authors concluded that all of the children had the opportunity to "participate in interactions with others in which what they do is prompted, responded to, prohibited, or affirmed."

The five-hundred-pound gorilla in these homes, they concluded, was not the kinds of experiences provided, but

> in the differing amounts of those experiences. The basic finding is that children who learn fewer words also have fewer experiences with words in interactions with other persons, and they are also children growing up in less economically advanced homes. Why do children differ so drastically in the trajectories of their word learning? It turns out that frequency matters. (Hart and Risley 1995, xiv–xv)

[Remember, we are talking about instruction here—as always, broadly defined—thus this last phrase can be restated as "amount of instruction matters."]

The data were parsed in many different ways that can't be done justice here. For example, in addition to the total frequency of parental communication, five characteristics thereof were defined and quantified:

1. Number of different nouns and modifiers a parent said per hour (language diversity);
2. Proportion of feedback to the child that was positive (feedback tone);
3. Proportion of communication comprised of nouns, modifiers, and past-tense verbs (symbolic emphasis);
4. Proportion of communication involving asking the child something rather than being told to do something (guidance style); and
5. Proportion of parental communication in response to the child's utterances rather than being parentally initiated (responsiveness).

The children were formally tested twice, once at age three and once at age nine. Age three variables were:

1. Vocabulary growth modeled over time,
2. Vocabulary use, and
3. IQ (conceptualized as a measure of the amount a child had learned up to that point, rather than a static measure of innate ability).

Then, for the twenty-nine nine- to ten-year-old third-grade children for whom the data were available, performance measures included administering standardized tests consisting of (a) vocabulary/language skills, and (b) basic academic skills. Statistical analyses revealed that family background variables (social-status categories, education, and income) were related to the parental communication indicators, especially frequency. Or, in the authors' words:

> The link between the parents' income, education, and social status, and their children's academic test performance had declined by the third grade. However, the link between what the parents were doing with their children before the children were three years old remained as strong as ever over the intervening six years ($p < 0.001$). (Hart and Risley 1995, 162)

The authors summed up the primary lesson they learned from their study (and hence a finding that all educational researchers engaged in this genre of research [and all parents in general] should be aware of) as follows:

> we also learned that the problem of intervening in the lives of children from families in poverty is considerably more complex than we thought, simply because the first 3 years of experience are so much more important than we thought. (Hart and Risley 1995, 168)

No study is without flaws and this one suffered from the possibility that parents might have behaved differently when they were being observed, as well as the relatively small sample size. Projections based upon actually observed time (in this case one hour per month) to total unobserved time are also always tenuous. However, the general findings (as opposed to the point estimates) and their interpretation were unassailable and quite astonishing. (Furthermore, any educational researcher designing an observational study should read the methods section of "Meaningful Differences in the Everyday Experiences of Young American Children" to obtain an appreciation for the difficulties in, and the necessary steps required for, protecting the integrity of their data and ensuring its reliability.)

Somewhat sadly, Todd Risley (who died in 2007, followed by Betty Hart in 2012) marveled that the study was never replicated. The study is probably not even mentioned today in many educational research classes, which is comparable to majoring in psychology without ever hearing of Sigmund Freud or John Watson. And this is perhaps one of many reasons why no one recognizes education as a science: if we don't appreciate our own science why should anyone else?

Implications: There are three for this study that deserve mention:

1. Far and away the most important is the sheer amount of instruction some children receive prior to enrolling in school than others. *There is no conceivable way that this gap can be overcome by conventional classroom instruction* in which all children spend the same amount of time in the classroom.
2. This huge instructional deficit is why well-meaning societal programs such as Head Start have failed to make a substantive dent in the performance gap separating children of different ethnic and economic strata. It is also why such programs' initial positive learning effects decrease until they virtually disappear after a few years of schooling.
3. As Betty and Todd have warned us, the early years are far more important educationally than is commonly realized and even more difficult to intervene within. This doesn't mean that educational researchers shouldn't make the attempt, because if significant amounts of additional instruction aren't continued over significant periods of time these efforts will in the end be disappointing and fleeting.

GENRE #4: SCHOOL-BASED, DESCRIPTIVE/ OBSERVATIONAL STUDIES

This is another genre of research whose time has probably largely come and gone—*at least until we make substantive changes in the classroom model itself.* As mentioned previously, we already know just about everything we need to know about a teacher standing in front of twenty-five or so students possessing varying amounts of prior learning experiences. And certainly we don't need more studies such as those involving "whiteness" or "opportunity hoarding" highlighted earlier.

With that said, however, one of the most enlightening and well-done studies in the history of the science is a member of this genre. And since it provides perhaps the strongest evidence for the importance of *relevant instructional time*, it too will be abstracted in some detail. But perhaps its length is excusable since it may be the most important *schooling* study ever performed.

The Beginning Teacher Evaluation Study

Charles Fisher, David Berliner, Nikola Filby, Richard Marliave, Leonard Cahen, and Marilyn Dishaw (Editors: Lieberman and Denham 1980)

This fascinating, complicated, and most assuredly seminal study was initiated by the California Commission for Teacher Preparation and Licensing and funded by the National Institute of Education (a precursor to the current Office of Education). Its original purpose was to identify generic teacher competencies and evaluate teacher-education programs. Initial fieldwork performed between 1973 and 1976 suggested a different course of action. (Jim Popham [1971] and Bill Moody and colleagues [1973] and the present author [1973] could have saved them some time since we had all found that student achievement was unrelated to teacher training or experience, but sometimes researchers need to find out things for themselves.) Marjorie Powell (1980) described the initial phase of the project as follows:

> During 1974–1975, a pilot study was recommended to clarify a major concept emerging from the research: *instructional time* [italics added]. The research staff also recommended additional work to develop (1) tests of student achievement that were more sensitive to instruction than commercial standardized tests [which will shortly be introduced as our third Education Urban Legend] and (2) simpler and more accurate instruments for collecting time information from teachers. (Powell 1980, 4)

Fortuitously, this work was successfully accomplished and data collection for the primary study began two years later. The resulting, revised study would have been education's equivalent to the discovery of the double helix if education had ever developed into a real science with an actual agenda, but, alas, we know there were "many slips twixt" those lips and that cup.

After the classroom observation measures had been refined to match the schools' curriculum, the final phase of the study involved the meticulous observation of a sample of 261 second- and fifth-grade students enrolled in twenty-five second- and twenty-five fifth-grade classrooms. This sample was comprised of only those students in the midrange of ability within each classroom. This may appear to be an unusual decision but it was made to mitigate the third of the three problems previously identified as bedeviling educational research (i.e., the excessive variability between and within classrooms).

In addition, three types of classrooms were also purposefully chosen, but this time to ensure as wide a range as possible of classroom practices. Specifically, classrooms were chosen where student achievement in math and reading (the two subject matters under investigation) were exceptionally high, average, and exceptionally low. This was done in order to maximize potential differences in teacher behavior.

The students and their teachers were then observed for one complete day per week for twenty weeks from October to May. These intensive and repeated observations of the fifty classrooms were performed by trained field-workers who recorded:

1. The amount of time teachers allocated to instruction;
2. Student engagement rates; and
3. The degree to which the instruction assigned to individual students was appropriate (i.e., was either too easy or not too difficult to be performed with a reasonable degree of success).

With respect to teaching time, the overall second-grade results were as follows (the fifth-grade results were similar):

1. Two hours and fifteen minutes of the second-grade school day were devoted to academic activities (defined as instruction in reading, mathematics, science, and social studies);
2. Fifty-five minutes were devoted to nonacademic activities (such as music and art); and
3. Forty-four minutes were "wasted" on things such as waiting for assignments and conducting class business.

Of the slightly over two hours of instruction administered by the twenty-five second-grade teachers, the investigators found that the students themselves were actually engaged in learning for one hour and thirty minutes (or 71 percent of the time). What was far more telling, however, was the fact that the top 10 percent of the teachers allocated fifty minutes more to instruction than did the bottom 10 percent of teachers, and these top teachers' students were differentially engaged for about the same amount of extra time (fifty minutes). Extrapolating to the entire school year, the investigators estimated that the students of some teachers could receive 150 hours more instruction than the students of other teachers. And this in turn meant that some children received 71.4 days more instruction, or a total of over fourteen weeks of extra schooling!

With respect to the test results the investigators found that:

1. "The amount of time that teachers allocate to instruction in a particular curriculum content area is positively associated with student learning in that content area." (Powell 1980, 15)
2. "The proportion of allocated time that students are engaged is positively associated with learning." (Powell 1980, 16) (Engagement was quantified by observing the amount of time the selected students were "on task" or "paying attention" to the instruction.)

3. "The proportion of time that reading or mathematics tasks are performed with high success is positively associated with student learning." (Powell 1980, 16) [Highly successful performance on a task was defined in terms of whether or not the student could perform the task while making only "occasional careless errors." Low success was defined in terms of the student supplying correct responses only at (or slightly above) chance levels.]

In an attempt to put some of their findings into a more understandable schooling/testing context, the investigators contrasted two hypothetically average students, one of whom (Student A) received a grand total of four minutes per day of relevant instruction, and one (Student B) who received fifty-two minutes. Since these students were indeed average (recall that "average" students were targeted by the study in the first place), both would begin the school year at the fiftieth percentile on a standardized achievement test. By midyear, however, Student A would have declined to the thirty-ninth percentile, while Student B would have improved to the sixty-sixth percentile!

A quasi-replication: It would be inexcusable not to mention another seminal observational study published in the same year as the *Beginning Teacher Evaluation Study* and which may be an equally seminal contribution to the science. This effort, called the *Instructional Dimensions Study* (Cooley and Leinhardt 1980) was (a) also designed to ascertain the relationship between instructional practices and student achievement and (b) also involved observations conducted in an almost unbelievably large sample of four hundred classrooms selected from one hundred different schools.

Some of its authors' conclusions resonate over the more than three succeeding decades and also emphasize the preeminent importance of the *amount* of direct, *relevant* academic instruction as the predominant determinant of student achievement. A sample of Cooley's and Leinhardt's findings and conclusions follow:

1. The most pronounced trend in these data, the importance of opportunity to learn (defined in terms of percentage of students on task and whether what was taught overlapped with what was tested [i.e., comparable to the "academic learning time" of the *Beginning Teacher Evaluation Study* and "relevant instructional time" here]) suggests that the most useful thing to do for children with underdeveloped reading and mathematics skills in the primary grades is to provide more direct instruction in these areas. . . . *It seems clear that what gets taught is a more important consideration than how it's taught* [italics added]. (Cooley and Leinhardt 1980, 22)

2. *When certain ends are met, such as regular assessment of student mastery and attention to individual student needs, the question isn't how it's done, but that it is done in some fashion* [italics added once more and the present

author's favorite quote from a research study]. (Cooley and Leinhardt 1980, 22)

A Lamentation

Isn't it odd that none of the recent value-added diatribes mentioned the findings of either *The Beginning Teacher Evaluation* or *The Instructional Dimension*? Practitioners of a real science such as physics would be astounded by such an omission (or perhaps simple ignorance of their discipline's past). After all, Newton graciously attributed much of his success to being able to stand on the shoulders of past "giants" in his field and Einstein claimed he would have never conceived the theory of general relativity without James Clerk Maxwell's work.

There were other voices repeating this message regarding the importance of relevant instructional time during this 1980s golden era of schooling research (largely ignored at the time and now long forgotten) as well—such as Jere Brophy's (1986) summing up of two decades of research on effective instruction:

> Students achieve more when their teachers emphasize academic objectives in establishing expectations and allocating time, *use effective management strategies to ensure that academic learning time is maximized*, pace students through the curriculum briskly but in small steps that allow high rates of success. (Brophy 1986, 1069)

Implications: These two monumental investigations (*The Beginning Teacher Evaluation* and *The Instructional Dimension Studies*) provide just about the strongest possible evidence for the importance of both instructional time and ensuring its relevance imaginable. They were positioned *after* the discussion regarding the sound and fury rigamarole surrounding the value-added teacher evaluation fad for two reasons.

First, while tomes were written supporting and attacking this latter fad, none read by the present author (who read a great many of them) ever mentioned either of these studies despite the fact that they were high-quality, definitive studies that would have definitively identified the behavioral etiology of value-added effects on achievement were these effects to have existed (which they may well have, just not reliably enough to inform any sensible policy).

Second, no one pays any attention to educational researchers—not educators, not politicians, not the public, and especially strikingly, not educational researchers themselves. (And even if a few enlightened members of the latter group were interested in anything besides their own work, their institutional memory is so brief that everything is forgotten in a decade.)

So perhaps this chapter should have been titled *"Four Genres That Should Have Been Useful, But Weren't."* But regardless of how they are described, all four genres are primarily historical in nature. We don't need to keep reinventing the wheel and naming it something else. What we need to do is change the predominant schooling paradigm. (What that change needs to entail will be discussed in this book's companion volume.)

But in the meantime, let's continue our whirlwind tour with a consideration of three research genres that probably should be discontinued (one of which has actually impeded the development of the science).

Chapter 4

Three Research Genres That Were Never Useful and Should Be Abandoned

The first of these genres has been by far the most detrimental to the development of a useful science of education. It involves a major misconception that turned out to be a mega-mistake for the science of education and therefore will be introduced via our third education urban legend:

Education Urban Legend #3: *Standardized Achievement Tests Are Sensible Measures of School Learning and Are Useful for Research Purposes.* They are neither.

RESEARCH GENRE #5: PSYCHOMETRIC RESEARCH

The majority of modern psychometric research involves tomes of minutia published in myriad journals; articles as relevant to learning instruction as counting the number of angels dancing on pinheads (and then describing the characteristics of each dancer in excruciating detail). It all is, in other words, completely irrelevant to the education or assessment of children and won't be discussed here.

What is very relevant are the types of tests we rely upon to evaluate student progress, teacher quality, school performance, and even to compare the educational systems of different countries. All of these tests are based upon a more-than-century-old psychometric model developed for a completely different purpose and bequeathed to us by our parent discipline.

From one perspective, our initial adoption of this model was quite understandable because education suffers from a major scientific disadvantage compared to its physical and biological counterparts. Education has no single quantifiable indicator of learning comparable to these disciplines such as weight, heat, brightness, or cell counts—all of which can be specified in terms of absolute *amounts*. True, we can indicate how many items a student answers correctly on a specific test or how many more items our intervention groups answer correctly than their controls.

We can also attach *p*-values to these differences regarding how many times such a result would occur by chance alone just like our more fortunate natural science cousins. But clinically, how do we quantify how *much* a student has learned over the course of a school year? Presently we can't even sensibly report how many *more* items students in any given school answered correctly in the spring of one year versus the spring of the preceding year since different tests were administered with different items and often different numbers of items.

So the early twentieth-century intelligence-test developers entered our story—those worthy successors of the science of craniology, a disproportionate number of both schools of whom were avowed eugenicists. But ignoring politics, these psychologists were faced with an interesting and daunting problem. True, long before anyone developed a test for it, everyone already knew what intelligence was, who had it, and especially who didn't.

Educated individuals were intelligent, uneducated individuals were not. The rich were, the poor weren't (especially if their grammar was different from nonstandard English). Blacks and recent immigrants weren't either (since they had had little access to education or exposure to the "proper" grammatical style during childhood).

But unfortunately, despite this important knowledge, scientists (and psychologists in particular) hadn't been able to credibly quantify the construct since the prevailing theory (craniology) of the day and metric (head circumference, which involved an honest-to-goodness indicator of *amount*) proved to be worthless after decades of research. So gradually, the paradigm began to change and instead of physical measurement (which was so successful in the natural sciences and responsible for much of their truly impressive successes up to that point and thereafter), "mental" measurement became increasing popular.

And given the unassailable knowledge of what intelligence was (namely that it was an immutable attribute that some people had more of than others), it was pretty much taken for granted that intelligence had to be a single entity that could be measured by a test of *some* sort.

Consequently, the most-influential early intelligence-test developers purposefully constructed their measures to reflect this single factor construct and christened it "g" (general) via a classic self-fulfilling prophesy. They also selected tasks and items that weren't customarily part of the standard school curriculum since intelligence, being immutable, shouldn't be influenced by learning. All of which conveniently allowed these early psychologists to decree that the end result of their tests couldn't be taught (therefore moving a step closer to a self-fulfilling prophesy). And intelligence itself could be defined as "intelligence is what the tests test" (Boring 1923, 35), which was definitely several steps past a self-fulfillment prophecy into something resembling a religion.

A Quick, But Not Completely Irrelevant Aside

The developers of the Scholastic Aptitude Test (SAT) adopted a very similar stance until relatively recently, claiming that their test couldn't be taught based upon their decision to include many items that weren't part of many public schools' curricula, especially in high schools serving lower socioeconomic families. However, once the evidence for the success of commercial SAT-preparation courses (which taught both test-taking skills and test content) became completely irrefutable, the test marketers finally dropped that claim since just about every student whose parents could afford it enrolled in these courses. (And public schools serving populations that couldn't afford the commercial preparation courses began to offer their own watered-down versions thereof.)

Perhaps partly due to this, partly to the growing political incorrectness of terms such as "ability," "intelligence," and "aptitude," the corporations involved (The College Board and the Educational Testing Service) changed the name of the test to the SAT Reasoning Test, but upon discovering that the new name carried much of the same connotations as the original, they simply changed the name of the test to what everyone called it anyway, the SAT.

In testing, as in many marketing enterprises, names are very, very important. Important enough to be shortly awarded not one, but two, of the book's upcoming Bogus Assessment Principles!

Nowhere is the history of the intelligence-testing industry (and the even larger "achievement testing" industry it spawned) is this better illustrated than in the work of the French psychologist Alfred Binet who, after becoming disillusioned with craniology, used many of these principles to develop his now-famous IQ test. Not pretending to know exactly what to include in his test, he simply punted and declared:

It matters very little what the tests [tasks or items] *are as long as they are numerous.* [Attributed to Alfred Binet in the Mismeasurement of Man (Gould 1981, 145)]

This transparent (or arrogant, depending upon one's perspective) admission/decision had a number of largely unrecognized implications, many of them antithetical to education in general and learning specifically. First, the tasks included had to be "numerous" because the more tasks or items any test contains, the more stable the scores produced become. This is called the *reliability* of a test and it means, among other things, that if the test is administered twice to the same group of individuals their scores will be very similar both times. (That is, the correlation between the two sets of scores administered to the same individuals will be quite high.)

Second, as arrogant and confident as many intelligence-test developers were in those early days, none probably believed that they knew all of the disparate characteristics that comprised human intelligence. So obviously it was impossible to specify the *amount* of intelligence possessed by any given individual.

But what they could do is test large numbers of individuals who were relatively representative of the population as a whole. These scores could then be rank ordered from low to high, which in turn permitted the percentage of people who scored above and below any given score to be calculated.

This process was facilitated greatly by a very useful mathematical model that we all know now as the normal or bell-shaped curve. This in turn allowed simple algebraic manipulations to give any scores any desired, intuitive metric the test developers chose. And thus was born the IQ scores with the average score being arbitrarily set to 100, which in turn allowed even the most mathematically challenged parents and educators to immediately ascertain whether any child of any background was above or below average intelligence.

Other tests were given other arbitrary values (e.g., such as 500 for the average SAT math and critical reading scores), and all could be converted to percentiles that told the exact rank any given person achieved on whatever the test purported to measure.

It was this psychometric model, given a steroidal boost by administering intelligence tests to millions of American soldiers in our two world wars, that was eagerly adopted by commercial achievement tests and thus became the standard representation of learning in both the public schools and educational research. And that, Dear Reader, is what we owe these early twentieth-century misanthropes (and here Binet should be given a pass, since his original motivations were to develop a test to identify children at risk for later school failure and then provide them with *additional* instruction).

So now it was not only possible to rank order people, but cut points could be created for different ranges of scores and labeled any way the test developers pleased. (The early intelligence experts preferred terminology such as "genius," "idiot," "imbecile," and so forth, but for some reason these names have fallen out of professional favor.)

So even though education is a strikingly different science with a radically different agenda than psychology, until relatively recently educators believed that intelligence was immutable and not influenced by instruction. Learning, on the other hand, is an extremely mutable construct subject to immediate change in the presence of instruction. (We know now, of course, that intelligence, like "aptitude," can also be *taught* [see Nisbett (2009) for an excellent nontechnical review of this issue.])

More crucially, however, while we will probably never be able to quantify the *amount* of intelligence any given individual possesses (nor is there really any reason to so anyway), we *can* specify the *amount* of learning students have *acquired* if we choose a suitable metric such as the number of (a) instructional objectives mastered, (b) words recognized, or (c) multiplication facts memorized.

We could also (with a bit more difficulty) specify the average amount of instructional *time* the mastery of specific instructional objectives requires and thereby estimate how much additional instruction an individual will need to master any give curriculum. Both the number of instructional objectives mastered and time are objective measures of quantity, not unlike the types of measures used in the biological (e.g., height, weight, age, heart rate) or physical (e.g., pressure, force, time, distance, or speed).

However, since current commercial achievement tests are developed via the same psychometric model as intelligence tests were over a century ago, they emphasize two rather bizarre and antiquated constructs. The most objective of these constructions is called *reliability* (i.e., the *stability* of a test) which ironically is antithetical to the measurement of learning since reliability is increased when test items are answered correctly by only about 50 percent of the test takers and when there are a lot of them (or "numerous" using Binet's vocabulary).

Thus a test with items that almost everyone will answer either correctly or incorrectly will possess extremely low reliability and is therefore considered to be a "bad" test in psychometric terms. This, of course, is at odds with the very purpose of *instruction*, which is to ensure that as many students as possible answer as many test questions correctly as possible. Very brief tests also tend to have low reliabilities, even if only a few items can quite adequately ascertain whether a concept has been learned or not.

The second psychometric concept (also unfortunate from a learning assessment perception) is called *test validity*. It is most commonly defined in terms of whether or not the test measures what it purports to measure, but there are so many manifestations of it (e.g., construct, concurrent, predictive, content, face, factorial) that no one pays much attention to it other than to accept corporate (or investigator) assurances that their tests have it.

The original intelligence-test developers emphasized factorial validity to support their conceit that intelligence was a single entity or "thing," but we now know that there are probably at least eight types of intelligence (Gardner 1983), so any subscriber to William of Occam's parsimony edict (of which the present author is definitely a devotee) would challenge the utility or use-fulness of both these multifaceted concepts (i.e., intelligence *and* validity).

Perhaps the most commonly used facets of validity today are its *concurrent* (defined in terms of one test's correlations with another) and *content* manifes-tations. For achievement tests, these are respectively defined in terms of (a) the test's ability to rank ordering students similarly to other achievement tests (surely another self-fulfilling prophesy) and (b) the test items matching the curriculum (which is surely a *good* thing for any test of learning). However, we already know what the father of intelligence testing (Alfred Binet) thought of content validity: it doesn't matter what the items are as long as there are enough of them.

But what are we to make of the fact that intelligence tests and learning tests share so many common factors and basically rank students similarly (i.e., are cor-related) with one another? If William of Occam were alive today (and he could be convinced that psychology and education were actually sciences) he would probably present the following conclusion based upon the following arguments:

1. Since achievement tests administered before children are admitted to school correlate highly with achievement after enrollment therein,
2. Since a large proportion of these relationships are due to the home envi-ronment, which equate to extra instruction,
3. Since both intelligence and achievement are influenced by the amount of instruction (a great deal of it occurring prior to school enrollment), *then*:
4. The correlation between the two are due to instruction (broadly) defined, *hence*
5. Intelligence and learning aren't separate constructs and both are a result of instruction (broadly defined).

Similarly, since reliability and validity are integrally related (i.e., if a measure isn't sufficiently stable [reliable] it won't correlate with anything [validity of the predictive or concurrent flavor]), Barker of Maryland might further suggest that:

1. Psychometricians should go back to the drawing board (or retreat back deep into the bowels of academia and leave the measurement of learning alone), and
2. Educational researchers should concentrate their efforts on developing test items based solely upon the curriculum and those behaviors the cur-riculum is designed to facilitate (hence not writing items based upon their difficulty but upon their appropriateness).

But perhaps we are getting a little off message here because this book is about science, not policy, and fads and education urban legends of the man-bites-dog genre are the stuff of educational policy. (How such tests can be developed is covered in this book's companion volume.)

Also, changing the testing system will be a hard sell. Our current testing model is something that many, many people believe in. It is attractive to politicians because they know the schools are failing a large swath of low-income children but they don't know what to do about it except to continue to test them. It is attractive to educators because nothing is held more dearly than what we have been taught and learned. And all educators have been indoctrinated in the power of the normal curve and the singular beauty of standardized tests.

However, everyone interested in education should at least be aware of the pseudo-mystical discipline that has grown up around the testing industry and avoid some of its more deleterious practices. In way of review, four of the most common of these practices follow:

Bogus Assessment Principle #1: *Ignore the items and you can call the test anything.* The *items* are *what* are actually being measured.

Bogus Assessment Principle #2: *Algebra can render otherwise noninterpretable test scores meaningful.*

Some tests have unique "points" or categories selected for them to make them more appealing and seemingly unique, such as 100 for IQ or 500 for SATs, but they are all cut from the same cloth and are nothing more than smoke screens.

Bogus Assessment Principle #3: *The stability (reliability) of a learning test is its most crucial characteristic and a prerequisite for its utility.*

Learning is a dynamic process subject to immediate change as a result of instruction, so measures used to assess how much students learn (or as research outcomes) should not be developed to maximize reliability. Instead, they should be developed to reflect the content of instruction and be as sensitive to change as possible. Changing the measurement model (e.g., from classic measurement to item-response theory or others being constantly invented) changes nothing but the terms and the algebraic formulas employed.

Bogus Assessment Principle #4: Writing a set of items to measure something, naming it, and correlating it with something else means (a) that the resulting instrument measures the construct its developer says it measures and (b) that the targeted construct exists.

Some aspect of this principle has served as the justification for most psychological variables as well as most *self-reported* educational questionnaires that purportedly tap such constructs as engagement, motivation, self-esteem, self-concept, self-efficacy, central executive, phonological loop, attitudes, aptitudes, intelligence, and perhaps hundreds of others. Not only is there no guarantee that these questionnaires measure what they are called, there is no guarantee that many of the constructs even exist (or even if they do and if they are educationally worthwhile).

To illustrate some of the problems associated with our third education urban legend (the misconception that standardized achievement tests are a measure of the amount of learning achieved), the following example is proffered preceded by our fourth education urban legend.

An Example of the Discipline's Inexhaustible Love Affair with Commercial Standardized Tests and the Education Urban Legend Which Follows It

Translating the Statistical Representation of the Effects of Education Interventions into More Readily Interpretable Forms

M. Lipsey, K. Puzio, C. Yun, et al. (2012)

The primary purpose of this monograph (funded by the US Department of Education) was a thorough explication of the different effect sizes (ESs) available to clinicians and researchers and the relationships between them, which the authors accomplished in exemplary fashion. (A reasonable objective, since there are many different manifestations of the ES and it is quite useful in determining an optimal sample size necessary to achieve statistical significance [another ordinal statistic] for a proposed experiment.)

Unfortunately, a second purpose was to suggest the use of standardized test benchmarks by which the practical utility and size of intervention effects can be evaluated. This objective is based on a previous, rather creative analysis (Bloom et al., 2008) in which the investigators:

> computed standardized mean difference effect sizes for year-to-year growth from the national norming studies performed by testing companies using nationally representative samples to create standardized percentile ranks (and other standardized score representations) for their tests] for standardized tests of reading, math, science, and social studies. Those data show the growth in average student achievement from one year to the next, growth that reflects the effects of attending school *plus the many other developmental influences students experience during a year of life* [italics added]. (p. 26)

The authors suggested that these results be employed as benchmarks to address, among other things, comparisons with other interventions and subgroups of students (such as the black–white achievement gap, or inner-city vs. suburban test results) that employed other achievement-related variables

On the surface this was a rather creative idea, but it assumes that these commercial tests accurately reflect students learning growth from year to year—a daunting task for any test to measure, but an assumption that apparently doesn't give most educational researchers (or educators) pause. Hopefully, however, following serious reflection it should strain anyone's credibility to assume that a single ordinal number that does not assess the *amount* of anything can capture a child's yearly growth, much less reflect the true extent of the so-called black–white or inner-city–suburban achievement gap. R-E-A-L-L-Y?

Especially since the ES is just another manifestation of bogus assessment principle #2 (*algebra can render otherwise noninterpretable test scores meaningful*), which converts a mean difference between two groups with zero reflecting no difference and 1.0 reflecting a difference equal to a standard deviation of one.

So with that in mind, here are the results emanating from the abovementioned norming data.

Annual Achievement Gain: Mean Effect Sizes across Seven Nationally Normed Tests

Hopefully, a close examination of this table would suggest that something is very, very wrong here. Let's graph the math achieve trajectory in way of illustration (see Figure 4.1), since all of the other subjects reflect the same rather nice, negatively linear trend:

First, does anyone believe that the ES of 0.01 (representing 1/100th of a standard deviation) reflects the *amount* the average high-school mathematics student learns in the eleventh grade? Or that an ES of 0.038 (the average of all four eleventh-grade content areas) reflects the totality of eleventh-grade *learning*?

Now admittedly, very few people examine statistical tables such as this closely, and even fewer have an intuitive understanding of what an ES of 0.01 represents. From an ordinal perspective, however (which is the only perspective yielded by an ES or any standardized score based upon the normal

Table 4.1 Annual Achievement Gain: Mean Effect Size Across Seven Nationally Normed-tests

Grade Transition	Reading	Math	Science	Social Studies
K–1	1.52	1.14	—	—
1–2	0.97	1.03	0.58	0.63
2–3	0.60	0.89	0.48	0.51
3–4	0.36	0.52	0.37	0.33
4–5	0.40	0.56	0.40	0.35
5–6	0.32	0.41	0.27	0.32
6–7	0.23	0.30	0.28	0.27
7–8	0.26	0.32	0.26	0.25
8–9	0.24	0.22	0.22	0.18
9–10	0.19	0.25	0.19	0.19
10–11	0.19	0.14	0.15	0.15
11–12	0.06	0.01	0.04	0.04

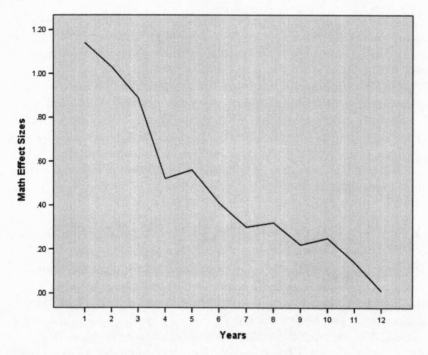

Figure 4.1   Math Standardized Achievement Test Yearly Gains Expressed as ESs. *Source*: Figure based upon data presented in Table 5 of Lipsey, Puzio, Yun, et al. (2012).

curve), an ES of 0.01 indicates that in a large high school with five hundred eleventh graders, only one student learned any math (as defined by the standardized math test) over the course of the school year!

For some reason, Dr. Lipsey and his colleagues neglected to mention this rather absurd fact, although he is well aware since he probably has written more about the ES (most of it quite sensible) than anyone of whom the present author is aware.

So taken at face value, wouldn't a reasonable *policy* implication of the results from this table be to abolish the eleventh grade (and undoubtedly the twelfth grade as well, assuming that this trend continues since twelfth graders would probably begin to learn less than zero [i.e., forget more than they learned])? Or if we believe that an ES really is a measure of *amount* of learning, that kindergarten students learn 114 times as much math as eleventh-grade students?

Or, given the IES paper's recommendation to use such ESs as benchmarks, wouldn't these data pretty much preclude conducting any type of learning experiments in middle school or high school where the average yearly achievement math gains are 0.28 and 0.13, respectively? To design a simple two-group experiment to produce such an ES using the eleventh-grade "benchmark" would require a sample size of over three hundred thousand to have an 80 percent chance of obtaining statistical significance (Bausell and Li 2002).

Naturally, there are more parsimonious and (heaven forbid) sensible explanations for all of this. Undoubtedly, the curriculum in the early grades is more restrictively defined and instruction therein more representative thereof. Hence the achievement tests are more representative of what is taught. In the upper grades, on the other hand, tracking is more common and the curriculum is more varied. And in high school, some students receive standard computational mathematics not dissimilar to what they've received in elementary school while others are exposed to advanced algebra and calculus.

A single test therefore cannot possibly cover such a diversity of subject matter. But if this is true, wouldn't another implication from all of this be that standardized tests are at best only proxies for learning and practically useless for experimental purposes? Or perhaps useless for *any* purpose?

What is obviously needed are learning tests capable of producing a discrete *score* that assesses the *amount* of learning acquired over a given segment of time in absolute terms, not a score that assesses how many students achieved a score higher or lower than said score. The technology for producing such tests already exists and consists of three components:

1. *Brief sets of items perfectly matching the relevant curriculum* (whether school-based or the instructional content of an experiment). The former have already been developed based upon the late Stan Deno's (1985) conception of *curriculum-based measurement.*
2. *Instructional objectives reflecting the curriculum being assessed.* Instructional objectives are elemental bits of instruction stated succinctly in behavioral terms and preferably accompanied by sample items that operationally define how mastery of an individual objective is to be assessed. They also fit nicely under the *curriculum-based* measurement umbrella and should be digitized to form the basis of all learning tests.

Implications: Until the demented commercial standardized-testing system is abolished, the present author can see no reason whatever for the continuance of business-as-usual psychometric research or the dozens of psychometric journals that continue to proliferate. There is a great deal of work required to convert to a *curriculum-based measurement* system, but we don't need psychometricians for that, just good item writers. (In this book's companion volume are some directions for future scientific work to accompany this proposed migration.)

All of which lead to the two most important educational assessment principles:

1. *Testing accompanied by immediate feedback is an extremely relevant form of instruction in and of itself.*
2. *The primary purpose of testing, and ultimately perhaps its only purpose from a learning perspective, is to inform instruction.*

Our current testing system completely ignores both principles. Commercial tests seldom report their results to guide-specific, individual instruction. And even if they did, these result aren't typically available until the school year is effectively over.

RESEARCH GENRE #6: META-ANALYSIS

This genre has already been mentioned in relationship to the huge size of the educational database. For our purposes, a meta-analytic study involves systematically searching for all of the empirical studies (published and unpublished) addressing the effects of a particular intervention upon student learning or achievement. Once located, the studies are then carefully reviewed, their results are translated into ESs, and a plethora of other study and design characteristics are normally coded. An overall ES (followed by many subgroup ESs) are then computed (normally weighted by the sample sizes associated with each individual ES) and analyzed somewhat similarly to the way individual ESs' results are statistically analyzed in an experiment in order to produce p-values and confidence intervals associated with whatever the analysts' research questions happened to be.

While the approach had been employed in medicine for several decades, Gene Glass introduced it to the educational research community by giving it its name (Glass 1976). He, with his wife (Glass and Smith 1979), also produced the discipline's first substantive educational example investigating the effects of class size. The procedure was eagerly adopted and the conduct of meta-analyses soon became a cottage industry that continues unabated to this day, with new ones typically being performed on older ones over and over again with minor variations.

The present author freely admits to being a huge fan of the technique when it was first proposed, advocated, and illustrated by Gene Glass. He also had no patience with critics arguing that combining the results of disparate studies was like mixing apples and oranges since educational experiments are more diverse than medical ones (where a meta-analysis often employs only randomized, placebo controled clinical trials involving the same diagnosis and outcome variable).

Unfortunately, this degree of specificity is not possible in education, with its different grade levels and diverse measures of the same subject matter (i.e., both different standardized and investigator-developed tests for each topic and grade level). Thus different meta-analyses or myriad subgroup (aka sensitivity) analyses must be computed to account for this diversity among students, design types, intervention differences, and so forth.

Also more problematic in education (present in medicine but to a lesser degree) is the fact that many high-impact journals tend to publish primarily statistically significant results (e.g., over 90 percent of the experiments published in the *Journal of Educational Psychology* report statistical significance in the predicted direction), which discourages investigators from even attempting to publish "negative" studies—thereby inflating meta-analytic ESs.

The first seminal meta-analyses of educational intervention meta-analyses (again, not a typo) of which the present author is aware was conducted by Mark Lipsey and his then-graduate student, David Wilson (1993), in which 302 meta-analyses of behavioral and educational interventions were located, only six of which reported numerically negative ESs and three of those were investigating the same topic.

However, by far the largest meta-analysis of *student achievement* meta-analyses was conducted twenty-five years later and involved not only interventions designed to improve achievement, but correlates thereof. This monumental effort is described in a book length monograph, a synopsis of which follows:

An Example of a Meta-Analysis Plus the Growth of Meta-Analysis as a Research Genre Plus an Illustration of the Vastness of the Educational Research Database Plus a Variation on Bogus Assessment Principle #2 (i.e., With a Simple Algebraic Manipulation [The ES]) We Can Combine Anything

Visible Learning: A Synthesis of Over Eight Hundred Meta-Analyses Relating to Achievement

John Hattie (2009)

The investigator divided 816 meta-analyses into six categories: student, home, school, teacher, curricula, and teaching effects. The average effect size of all six was 0.40 (very close to Lipsey and Wilson's average ES of 0.35 for educational intervention meta-analyses conducted two decades earlier, although again Hattie employed everything related to achievement, not just interventions).

This analysis represented 144,626 effect sizes (and as mentioned previously: 52,649 individual studies and 83,033,433 Ss) and he proportionally found even fewer negative ESs than Lipsey and Wilson.

While locating such an extensive list of meta-analyses (apparently, as of 2016, he had found slightly over a thousand such studies) constitutes a remarkable scientific contribution by itself (and synthesizing over eight hundred meta-analyses is a most daunting, ambitious, and time-consuming endeavor), the processes involved are vulnerable to several criticisms regardless of who conducts them. The more salient to our purposes follow.

What Hattie attempted to do was to synthesize (or make sense) of this welter of information—which in all fairness may have been an impossible task to begin with given the technique's (not to mention the original studies') deficiencies. He consequently categorized/compartmentalized this astounding abundance of data into the following four mega-categories:

1. Reverse effects (most of which were tautological in the sense that negative ESs represented positive effects such as the relationship between the amount of television watched and student achievement).
2. Maturation/developmental effects, which include ESs from zero (i.e., nonnegative) to 0.15 that Hattie claims "is what students could probably achieve if there was no schooling" (p. 20) (and is estimated from the findings in countries with no or limited schooling). This latter benchmark is, of course, utter nonsense.
3. Teacher effects, which include ESs from 0.15 to 0.40 "similar to what teachers can accomplish in a single year" (p. 20). Again, the basis for this is questionable given our discussion concerning the deficiencies inherent in both the ES concept and standardized tests.
4. Desired effects, which are any that produce an ES greater than 0.40 (hence any ES < 0.40 is apparently undesirable).

Based upon statistical significance, just about everything presently published in education "works," which makes one wonder how anyone could question the accomplishments of educational research. Or why so many of our schools appear to fail so many of their students. And especially why everyone ignores educational research.

Implications: While anyone who would collect and attempt to synthesize the results of 818 meta-analyses automatically gains entry into the present author's educational research hall of fame, this type of thinking reflects the systemic problems associated with both the ES concept and the meta-analytic process. Hattie's unquestioning faith in these approaches harks back to an analogy originally made by Jacob Cohen (1988) in which he (Hattie) characterized an ES of 0.29 as one which would not "be perceptible to the naked eye, and would be approximately equivalent to the difference between the height of a 5'11" (180 cm) and a 6'0" (182 cm) person" (Cohen 1988, 8).

While Cohen's place of honor in the hypothetical educational hall of fame is only an exhibition or two down the corridor from that of Edward Thorndike's, height (whether measured in feet and inches or centimeters) is an honest-to-goodness meaningful metric that doesn't need to be standardized on an ordinal scale in order to be interpreted. (As an aside, the average math standardized achievement ES for eleventh-grade students [Lipsey et al. 2012] would be the equivalent to less than 9 millimeters!]

And of course, even meta-analyses of meta-analyses (as well as meta-analyses of these meta-analyses of meta-analyses, which will almost surely be performed at some point if they haven't already) are subject to all of the other difficulties endemic to the genre, such as:

1. Publication bias (which is exacerbated because, while nonsignificant studies are underrepresented in the literature in the literature, investigators are even *less* likely to report studies with negative ESs (i.e., mean differences numerically favoring the control group);
2. Averaging extremely disparate entities (i.e., the apples-and-oranges analogy);
3. The inability to assess cumulativeness of interventions (since there is no easy way to assess whether two meta-analyses were mutually exclusive [e.g., that students receiving tutoring weren't also being assigned homework]); and
4. The fact that a collection of nonstatistically significant ESs can be combined to produce a highly significant meta-analytic conclusion.

So Are Meta-Analyses Completely Irrelevant?

A better question is: for what possible purposes are meta-analyses *not* completely irrelevant? In some cases, they can be helpful to researchers or product developers in identifying the type of work that has been done in a given area since as a group said researchers tend to be blissfully ignorant of past work. Also, even the ESs of individual studies can provide gross indications of efficacy, although never without close examination (including sensitivity/subgroup analyses).

But standing on their own (from either a practice or scientific perspective), it is difficult to ascertain any real utility of the genre for arriving at bottom-line conclusions or efficacy. Especially when the disadvantages stated above and the huge diversity characterizing the discipline experimental literature are taken into account. To illustrate (and delve into the genre in a bit more depth), let's examine what most professionals would consider an exemplary meta-analysis involving research on what is surely destined to become one of

the most prevalent forms of instruction in education with or without randomized trials or meta-analyses thereof:

An Exemplary (But as Always with This Genre, Less-Than-Satisfying) Example of a Meta-Analysis Comparing Intelligent Tutoring Systems with Other Instructional Methods

*A Meta-Analysis of the Effectiveness of Intelligent Tutoring Systems on K–12
Students' Mathematical Learning*

Saiying Steenbergen-Hu and Harris Cooper (2013)

This meta-analysis included twenty-six K–12 studies (thirty-four independent
samples) assessing the effectiveness of intelligent tutoring systems (ITS) on
math achievement. The authors concluded that "overall ITS had no negative
and perhaps a small positive effect on K-12 students' mathematical learning." The systems were compared to classroom instruction, human tutoring
(actually small-group instruction), and homework. Overall this produced
very small effect sizes (ranging from 0.01 to 0.09 depending upon the type of
analysis conducted and excluding sensitivity analyses).

However, the diversity among the ESs resulting from the sensitivity analyses was quite large (à la Disciplinary Problem #3: The excessive diversity
between and within educational settings coupled with the excessive number
of confounding variables accompanying the educational process) as witnessed by the subgroup results and their ESs in Table 4.2 below (abstracted
from Table 4.2 in the original article).

Thus to what settings or students can such disparate findings be applied by
a clinician or researcher? Especially since these categories are not mutually
exclusive and could therefore result in far more combinations of factors than
there are ESs if they were disaggregated? Or how could the subgroups even
be interpreted one at a time? For example, the older studies counterintuitively
produced significantly better results than the newer ones? Does this imply
that the software or hardware is becoming less effective over time? (Surely
the exact opposite is true.)

Some subgroup analyses are easier to interpret, such as the fact that studies published in peer-reviewed journals reported the highest ES of any other
category. This is a classic (and well documented) example of publication
bias, but of what use is such a finding other than a repetition of what we've
known for decades?

And to make matters worse, there was at least one other crucial variable
that wasn't included in the sensitivity analyses: type of curricular software
used. (Most were some version of Cognitive Tutor but six competing products in all were employed.)

Table 4.2   Selected Subgroup (Sensitivity) Analyses for ITS Meta-Analysis

Subgroup	N of ESs	ES	p-value
Duration of Intervention			
≥ 1 year	15	0.02	<0.001
< 1 year	11	0.23	
Grade Level			Not Significant
Elementary	3	0.21	
Middle	6	−0.001	
Secondary	14	0.06	
Research Design			<0.01
Quasiexperimental	15	0.09	
Randomized	11	−0.01	
Year of Data Collection			<0.001
Before 2003	7	0.27	
2003–2005	7	0.02	
2006–2010	8	−0.01	
Type of Test			<0.001
Standardized	20	0.02	
Course-related	16	0.19	
Report Type			<0.001
Peer-reviewed journal	10	0.28	
Nonjournal	16	0.02	

And while none of this is good news, the even worse news is that this diversity of studies is typical of the genre as a whole. And worse even than that, several other meta-analyses employing slightly different inclusion/ exclusion criteria reached disparate results (i.e., much larger ESs) compared to this one.

Implication/Conclusion: The same as was reached for psychometric studies: we *just don't need any more of the damn things.* But rest assured that there are going to be a *lot* more of them in our repetitive, unimaginative science ($p < 0.0001$).

RESEARCH GENRE #7: SCALE-UP EXPERIMENTS

These studies occur when an intervention has proved to be efficacious under controlled conditions, thereby motivating its introduction on a much larger scale under more veridical conditions. This approach usually entails depending upon school personnel to implement the innovation and/or monitor its continued use over time. Such studies are expensive and doomed to failure because:

1. They must typically employ large sample sizes, and more importantly,

2. Teachers and administrators have their own agendas, many of which entail
   simply getting through the day and not unnecessarily increasing their
   workloads by cooperating with researchers.

After all, one of the advantages of experience with a job is that it becomes
easier over time, while changing one's work routine is almost always more
difficult than continuing therewith. Back in the day, educational researchers
coined another principle equally as valid as the grandmother principle to
describe what happens to an instructional innovation, definitively proven to
be effective under controlled and carefully supervised conditions once it is
introduced into the classroom setting. It was called (please excuse the sani-
tization) the *excrement principle*, and like all good adages (or predictions) it
was quite succinct:

> *Everything turns to excrement in the traditional classroom.*

At one point, the Institute of Education Science seemed quite eager to fund
these studies and the results were a plethora of failures to "replicate." Probably no one is to blame for this since the entire profession is afflicted by a
severe long-term memory deficit.

Everyone who follows educational research now knows what the results
of scale-up experiments will be, but the next generation of researchers surely
won't so these studies will be repeated as long as the discipline continues to
be stuck in its circular trajectory. But in any event, we definitely don't *need* to
expend any more resources on this genre—a typical example of which follows.

An Example of What Happens When Teachers Decide When
and How an Implementation Will Be Implemented
(Or: Where Oh Where Did Our $14 Million Go?)

Effectiveness of Reading and Mathematics Software Products:
Findings from Two Student Cohorts

L. Campuzano, M. Dynarski, R. Agodini, and K. Rall (2009)

This large "scale-up" experiment compared sixteen reading and mathematics
software instructional systems to "conventional" classroom instruction using
standardized achievement tests as the outcome variable. Apparently, besides
ascertaining the overall effects of the software systems, part of the purpose
of the $14 million effort was to ascertain if teachers would indeed implement
the intervention. (Millions definitely aren't needed to answer that question.)

At experiment's end (data were collected over a two-year interval), no
statistically significant differences surfaced between the combined software

intervention and conventional classroom instruction. Not a particularly surprising finding, given that the intervention-group teachers opted to employ the software for an average of five minutes out of each fifty-minute class period.

When asked about the lack of implementation on the part of the experimental teachers, one of the investigators offered the following defense:

> We felt pretty confident that 10% of use reflects the sound judgment of the teacher about how often and for what kinds of instructional modules they wanted to use technology. (*Education Week*, April 11, 2007, p. 18)

The present author is far too refined to provide the appropriate rejoinder to this particular answer (or the wisdom of spending this amount of money to provide the grist for it). He also won't comment on the peer-review system that approved the funding of such a study. And, to be fair to everyone involved, there was ample support in the literature for the efficacy of computerized instruction, at least for those who accept meta-analytic results. Almost twenty years earlier, for example, one review of fifty-one studies evaluating computer-based teaching (Kulik, Bangert, and Williams 1983, 16) found that "the computer reduced substantially the *amount of time* [italics added] that students needed for learning."

Also, one would hope that a good deal of progress had been made in both computers and instructional software during that twenty-year time interval, but unfortunately not enough progress for five minutes per day of supplementary instruction to make any detectable difference! (Of course our previous meta-analytic example [Steenbergen-Hu and Cooper 2013] reached a somewhat different conclusion, but that's the nature of that beast and why meta-analyses are almost completely worthless for clinical decisions.)

What this study does demonstrate is the difficulty of getting any innovation or intervention *properly* implemented in the classroom paradigm as long as teachers are charged with said implementation. And that may be understandable, given the difficulties inherent in teaching a room full of diverse students, which is one reason educational research will never impact meaningful classroom change unless it reforms its own practices—either by helping to change (a) the classroom paradigm itself, (b) the way it conducts its research, or (c) the process by which boondoggles such as this are funded.

Chapter 5

Three Genres That *Could* Have Some Potential for Creating a Meaningful Science

Like Yogi Berra, the present author understands the difficulties of predicting the future, so the next three educational research genres won't be extolled over enthusiastically. However, regardless of any changes in the discipline's research agenda or funding levels, these genres are so conceptually appealing that studies therein will be conducted regardless of anything anyone says.

Like the previous three, a few have actually resulted in some potential minor improvements in the instructional process and perhaps some far-thinking investigators will do the same in the future. It may be, however, that most of the low-hanging fruit relevant to the obsolete classroom model has already been harvested.

GENRE #8: EXPERIMENTS CONDUCTED UNDER VERIDICAL SCHOOLING CONDITIONS

Since these studies will always be performed, our best hope is that "veridical schooling conditions" will eventually mean something very different than it does today. Until that day dawns, the most ambitious (and arguably one of the most influential) studies of its kind is abstracted below and constitutes the third pick for the top three or four educational research studies of all time. (And this one may even have been mentioned in some school of education courses.)

The State of Tennessee's Student/Teacher Achievement Ratio (STAR)

Elizabeth Word, John Johnston, Helen Pate Bain, B. DeWayne Fulton, Jayne Boyd Zaharias, Charles M. Achilles, Martha Nannette Lintz, John Folger, and Carolyn Breda (1994)

Funded by the state of Tennessee, over three hundred diverse elementary schools serving inner-city, suburban, urban, and rural families across the state with kindergarten enrollments of fifty-seven or more students were randomly assigned to one of three conditions:

1. A "regular size" classroom containing twenty-two to twenty-five students.
2. A "regular size" classroom employing a teacher aide.
3. A "small size" classroom containing fifteen to seventeen students.

The second condition (presence of a teacher aide) was employed to assess the possibility that the hypothesized effect for learning in small classes might be duplicated by supplying teachers with classroom help. (Hypothesized based upon the extremely influential meta-analysis [Glass and Smith (1979); see also Glass et al. (1982)] demonstrating the positive learning effects of smaller class sizes after years of controversy.) Unfortunately, teachers were allowed to use these aides in any way they saw fit, and the majority (predictably) did not use them for instructional purposes, such as small-group remediation or tutoring.

In the first year of the project (1985–1986), 128 small classes, 101 regular classes sans teacher aides, and 99 regular classes with aides were employed, containing approximately 1,900, 2,300, and 2,200 kindergarten students, respectively. Students were randomized within schools and continued to be taught in the same types of classrooms through third grade. The primary outcome variables consisted of math and reading scores on standardized and "curriculum" assessments.

The results were quite definitive: students in each grade level and each type of school registered greater math and reading gains in the small-class-size conditions than in regular-size classes (with or without an aide). Too many analyses (primary and secondary, longitudinal and grade-by-grade) were conducted to mention here, but the most interesting findings follow:

1. There was no statistically significant differential impact of small classes on whites or minorities (with both profiting significantly in comparison to large classes). In research, potential differential learning effects such as this are labeled aptitude-by-treatment interactions and they are so very, very rare that we'll award them the status of yet another Education Urban Legend shortly.
2. While students profited from small-classroom instruction in all four years, there was no cumulative effect for class size. (This was assessed by comparing students who continued to be enrolled in small classes versus those who did not—a rather weak contrast methodologically, since the two groups could well have differed on other learning-related factors.)

3. The effect for the teacher-aide condition as compared to no teacher aide was numerically (but not statistically) superior.

Follow-up: Funds were made available to determine if the achievement effects persisted over time in what was termed the Lasting Benefits Study. These analyses showed that the original experimental comparison persisted into grades 4 and 5 as reported in a conference paper (Achilles et al. 1993). Nye, Konstantopoulos, and Hedges (2004) claimed a similar effect at six years, and another set of authors (Finn, Gerber, and Boyd-Zaharias 2005) published an analysis a few years later purportedly showing that students who had been in small classes for three years had a higher graduation rate from high school. All of these later analyses (with the possible exception of the 1993 conference paper that could not be located) were conducted on subsets of the original sample due to significant student attrition, hence must be interpreted with caution.

Implications: Prior to Glass's seminal meta-analysis there had been a plethora of class-size studies conducted, with the majority showing no significant effects for smaller classes. (Some of these studies were as unsophisticated as comparing two undergraduate psychology sections that happened to have different size enrollments on a common final exam, but in general the effect was robust when design and other issues were taken into consideration.) While the Tennessee study supported the meta-analysis' results (a large, well-done, randomized trial always trumps a meta-analysis), and since everyone's grandmother already knew that small classes were "better" than large ones, this provided yet another confirmation of these ladies' wisdom and their revered scientific principle. And since teachers and parents also were cognizant of this fact, we have another definitive scientific demonstration of the obvious.

Despite the discipline's general acceptance of these results, many policy experts argued the size of the effect did not justify the intervention's cost (which in fairness would be quite high if it were to be implemented nationally). *No one*, economist or otherwise, knows how to balance cost (an actual, honest-to-goodness measure of *amount* since money can be *counted*) with standardized test scores (a measure comparing students with one another). Regardless, however, class sizes have tended to be reduced over time (often being one of the few sensible hallmarks of school-reform efforts as demonstrated in our next research genre) and this seminal study probably deserves some credit for that. (Given its age, this result does not qualify as evidence for or against the book's original thought question.) It is also supportive of our working hypothesis since smaller classrooms permit more relevant instruction to be administered (e.g., fewer disruptive behaviors and the possibility of more individualized instruction and feedback).

However, the future utility of this genre of research appears limited unless it involves the introduction of existing technology (already in use for other purposes) to substantively change the traditional classroom setting itself—a possibility that will be discussed in more detail in this book's accompanying volume.

GENRE #9: NATURAL EXPERIMENTS (EVALUATIONS) CONDUCTED WITHIN SCHOOLS

Experimental evaluation studies, sometimes called natural experiments, are often poorly designed and are more afterthoughts than true, prospective experiments such as the previous example. The study chosen to represent this genre certainly runs counter to this generalization, however, since it was well designed (if accidentally so) and has important implications for both the future of the science and our working hypothesis. (Evaluation/natural experiments are defined here as experiments in which the investigators do not implement the interventions, administer the outcome measures, and usually have little or no input in the experiment designs used although they often choose or constitute the comparison groups.)

As Example of a Natural Experiment Involving the Evaluation of an Exemplary Charter School

Are High-Quality Schools Enough to Close the Achievement Gap?
Evidence from a Social Experiment in Harlem

Will Dobbie and Roland G. Fryer, Jr. (2009)

As the beneficiary of a New York law requiring oversubscribed charter schools to allocate enrollment randomly via a lottery system, this study provided a relatively rare experimental opportunity to study the effects of these charter schools upon student achievement via a comparison of students (a) who won the lottery and attended the charter schools versus (b) students who applied but were randomly denied entrance.

Available standardized achievement tests mandated by the state were employed as the outcome variables. The design was also supplemented by nonrandomized comparisons with (a) students from adjacent geographic areas eight hundred, sixteen hundred, and twenty-four hundred meters outside the Harlem Children's Zone (HCZ); (b) achievement data on siblings of selected students who had not attended the charter schools; and (c) national norms (always an exceedingly weak comparator because of the previously noted deficiencies inherent in commercial standardized tests). In addition, supplementary intent-to-treat analyses were conducted contrasting all students who were offered a spot in the charter schools, whether they attended or chose not to attend, versus studed as offering:

> an extended school day and year, with coordinated afterschool tutoring and additional classes on Saturdays for children who need remediation in mathematics and English Language Arts skills. *Our rough estimate is that HCZ Promise Academy students that are behind grade level are in school for twice as many hours as a traditional public school student in New York City* [italics added]. Students who are at or above grade level still attend the equivalent of about fifty percent more school in a calendar year. (Dobbie and Fryer 2009, 6)

Armed with a strong and plausible rationale for why these schools should produce increased student learning (a massive dose of extra instruction supplemented by tutoring), the investigators used available middle-school data from this social experiment to "understand whether communities, schools, or a combination of the two are the main drivers of student achievement."

Both the randomized and nonrandomized comparisons resulted in the same finding:

> Harlem Children's Zone is effective at increasing the achievement of the poorest minority children. Students enrolled in the sixth grade gain more than four-fifths of a standard deviation in math and between one-quarter and one-third of a standard deviation in English Language Arts (ELA) by eighth grade. Taken at face value, these effects are enough to close the black–white achievement gap in mathematics and reduce it by about half in ELA. Students in the HCZ elementary school gain approximately four-fifths to one and a half a standard deviation in both math and ELA by third grade, closing the racial achievement gap in both subjects. (Dobbie and Fryer 2009, 2)

Whether the conclusions regarding the closure of the "black-white achievement gap" should be "taken at face value" is highly questionable, being yet another attempt to use an ordinal measure (the standardized ES) as an indicator of amount of learning. However, the positive intervention results as compared to the control group are not at all questionable.

Implications: There are several things to like about this study. It reflects an understanding that the governmentally prescribed amount of classroom instruction is not sufficient for children who begin school with the huge deficits in instructional time characterizing educationally deprived home environments. It also employs tutoring, which encompasses the most intense and relevant known form of instruction; therefore its success provides the strongest *experimental* support for out working hypothesis theory yet discussed. There is also a lot to like about the genre itself—but regardless of its potential for informing the science, empirical evaluations of politically mandated interventions will (and should) always be conducted. And hopefully they will be as exemplarily performed as this one. (Offering the intervention in an area in which it is sure to be oversubscribed and employing a randomized lottery system for participation should be always considered for such interventions.)

GENRE #10: EXPERIMENTS CONDUCTED IN SCHOOLS UNDER LABORATORY CONDITIONS (OR EXPERIMENTS DESIGNED TO ASCERTAIN "WHAT COULD BE" RATHER THAN "WHAT IS")

Our next genre of research has not had as much impact on the science as some of the preceding ones, but our disciplinary tour would be incomplete without it. This genre of experimental research is physically conducted in the schools but under considerably more controlled conditions than the conventional classroom permits. Its studies can extend from small-scale, inexpensive experiments of brief duration to large expensive ones extending over large portions of the school year. Because the instructional environment is created by the investigators to avoid the constraints imposed by the classroom paradigm, any results accruing from this genre belong to the realm of what *could be* rather than to the everyday world of *what is* or *is likely to be*.

Examples of the procedural control that this genre is able to bring to the scientific table include the ability to:

1. Ensure that the intervention is properly implemented. This is sometimes called *treatment fidelity* but it basically means that the investigators, not the classroom teachers, carefully control and document the implementation the intervention. Classroom teachers have other agendas and cannot be expected to (and will not typically) implement an intervention conscientiously that involves considerable effort on their part or that extends over any significant period of time. The most likely result is therefore no statistically significant difference between the innovation and its randomly assigned comparison group regardless of the intervention's efficacy or lack thereof.
2. Ensure that the curriculum is rigorously controlled so that the instruction in one condition does not match the outcome measure more closely than the other condition (which very often occurs when the latter is a comparison group euphemistically referred to as "usual instruction," "business-as-usual," or a synonym thereof). If the curriculum is not controlled, then the condition that more closely matches the achievement test will most likely prove to be superior—but will be scientifically meaningless.

3. Construct or select the learning outcome measure to match the experimental curriculum (which is rigorously adhered to by all of the experimental conditions). This in turn legislates against standardized commercial tests that are developed to span different school, district, and state curricula.

So please permit a large helping of self-indulgence and allow the present author to abstract a very old example of this genre of research. It probably had little or no significant impact upon the science and its results also did nothing to refute the grandmother principle.

But in the Authors' Defense, a Bit of Background

While tutoring was the schooling option of choice (and sometimes the only choice) for the privileged classes in the past, it appeared to be largely unappreciated in professional education circles prior to the late 1960s and early 1970s. Today it is a multibillion-dollar industry, with just about *all* university-bound students receiving tutoring at some point during their schooling career to (a) provide remedial instruction in a subject they are weak in, (b) compensate for substandard schools or classroom teachers, and/or (c) prepare them for the SATs.

An even higher percentage of students have received parental tutoring, whether prior to the advent of school, as an adjunctive form of instruction once enrolled, or both. (It could be argued, in fact, that the parenting process itself is the quintessential expression of tutoring.)

So given the context in the 1970s (i.e., a disinterest in tutoring among educators and educational researchers), the investigators of this experiment decided to provide a demonstration of the effectiveness of tutoring when *teacher effects, student differences, instructional time,* and *the curriculum* were rigorously controlled. They also felt constrained to proactively address two potential objections they were convinced that the critics of this study would raise: whether tutoring was equally effective for all types of students and the economic impracticality of employing trained, experienced teachers to tutor students.

A Demonstration of Tutoring's Superiority Over Classroom Instruction

A Factorial Study of Tutoring versus Classroom Instruction

R. Barker Bausell, William B. Moody, and F. Neil Walzl (1973)

The investigators described the rationale for the experiment via somewhat over-the-top prose as follows:

> Tutoring is one of the oldest variables in educational theory. Long before Emile, possibly before Plato, it was hypothesized to be superior to other instructional methods and class sizes. Despite this venerable history, tutoring as an educational variable has largely escaped empirical scrutiny in this century, due perhaps to its seeming impracticality. Despite practical constraints, however, supplementary or remedial tutoring is being increasingly employed within contemporary school systems with severely academically deficient children. Furthermore, the practicality of individual instruction has been increased in recent years by the advent of increased leisure time coupled with the realization that teacher training and experience do not appear to affect the amount children learn. (Bausell, Moody, and Walzl 1973, 591) [Two citations were presented for the latter statement: Popham (1971) and Moody and Bausell (1971).]

Pilot work was conducted in order to (a) select a curricular unit that could be taught in a brief instructional window and (b) construct a test sensitive enough to detect statistically significant learning gains after only thirty to forty minutes of instruction. (This brief instructional window was necessitated based upon time constraints dictated by the schools involved, advice presented in the Ellson Programed Tutoring Study [1965] to be discussed in the book's companion volume, and to permit close monitoring by the investigators of both the tutoring and classroom conditions to ensure fidelity to the experimental curriculum.)

In the end, an introductory unit on exponents was chosen in preference to probability and number theory based upon the students (a) scoring near zero on the pretest and (b) learning more of the objectives than the other two units when taught in a classroom setting by the second author. Eight objectives were consequently selected from a list of fifteen and the two best-functioning items measuring each objective were chosen, thereby producing a sixteen-item, short-answer test.

Undergraduate volunteers were solicited from two groups of school of education students: (a) those who had not received any college-level course work in teaching elementary-school mathematics or formal teaching experience, and those who had completed the relevant school of education courses and had almost completed their elementary-school practice teaching experience. One week before the experiment began, each of the undergraduate teachers was provided with a packet containing (a) the eight instructional objectives that they were to teach (e.g., "Rename the product of two numbers with like bases as the common base with an exponent equal to the sum of the two exponents."), (b) examples of the items used to assess mastery of each objective using the same open-ended format (but not the actual items), (c) a very brief mathematical rationale for each objective, and (d) instructions to teach all eight objectives as intensively as possible. (No other instructions were provided.)

The procedural components of the experiment were as follows:

1. The sixteen-item exponent test was administered as a pretest three days prior to the experiment. Only students who scored four or below were considered eligible for the experiment (slightly over 90 percent of the sample).
2. Within each of the preexisting classrooms within each of three schools, students were rank-ordered from high to low on their Primary Mental Abilities IQ scores. Each of the resulting lists of rank-ordered students was then divided into thirds, and the students within these thirds were defined as possessing high, medium, and low "abilities." The median for each third was identified, and the six students whose IQ scores were numerically closest thereto were selected for the study.
3. Within each school, each undergraduate teacher was randomly assigned two low-, two medium-, and two high-ability students of the same grade level. One student from each of these pairs was randomly assigned to receive tutoring, and the other student to receive classroom instruction. Each undergraduate teacher therefore (a) instructed one full classroom of students and (b) conducted three separate individual tutoring sessions with his or her randomly assigned high-, medium-, and low-ability students.

The targeted fourth- and fifth-grade students were tutored two days prior to classroom instruction. It would have been optimal to have counterbalanced the order in which tutoring vs. classroom instruction was delivered, but practical constraints precluded this. However, two of the investigators (Moody and Bausell 1971) had previously demonstrated that a teaching-practice effect for this experimental unit occurred only between the first and second tutoring sessions, not thereafter (at least not up to six sessions).

For the thirty-minute tutoring sessions, students were taken from their regular classroom activities by the investigators and placed in the charge of their assigned tutor in a quiet, isolated area within the building. The order in which each teacher's high-, medium-, and low-ability students were tutored was randomized for the fourth-grade students via a Latin Square design, although the order was not randomized for the fifth-graders due to a procedural glitch. (Subsequent analysis revealed no primacy effect for either grade level, however.)

Each undergraduate was thus randomly assigned within schools to one class of fourth- or fifth-grade students with the constraint that each undergraduate's six randomly assigned high-, medium-, and low-ability students were included therein (three that he or she had already tutored and the three matching students who had not been tutored). The undergraduate teachers were not aware of the experimental design or the existence of these matched students. They were simply told that their task was to promote class attainment of the eight objectives. All undergraduates then instructed their assigned classes in the instructional unit for the same amount of time (thirty minutes) as their tutoring sessions.

No specific teaching instructions were given to the undergraduates other than to spend all of their instructional time in teaching the eight objectives. All tutoring and classroom instruction settings were cursorily observed to ensure fidelity with the instructional protocol.

The exponents test was administered immediately following classroom instruction, although only data from the three embedded, randomly assigned students within each classroom were analyzed. The results were:

1. Tutored students learned significantly more than their randomly matched counterparts, who had been taught the identical content by identical teachers for an identical amount of time in a classroom setting.
2. The high-ability group scored significantly more on the posttest than medium-ability students, who in turn scored significantly higher than low-ability students in both the tutoring and classroom conditions.
3. Tutoring was equally effective for all three student-ability levels (i.e., there was no aptitude-by-treatment interaction).
4. There was no difference in the amount of student learning elicited between untrained, inexperienced sophomores and better trained, more experienced seniors. (Also, the two types of teachers did not differ with respect to their relative tutoring versus classroom effectiveness.)

Implications: On one level, the results were completely *obvious* and everyone's grandmother could have predicted that tutoring would be superior to classroom instruction. What most researchers would not have predicted, however, is how much more effective tutoring *can be* under meticulously controlled conditions than classroom instruction: namely that statistically significant learning differences could be observed in less than a single class period.

Also in the authors' defense, this was the first randomized controlled trial comparing tutoring with classroom instruction in which (a) instructional time, (b) the curriculum, (c) student differences, and (d) teacher differences were procedurally controlled. However, a case could be made that demonstrating the obvious does not constitute very meaningful science.

Tutoring versus small-groups instruction: The tutoring study was replicated and extended (Moody, Bausell, and Jenkins 1973) at the third author's (Jenkins) suggestion using a similar design. The exponent unit was again used (although ten objectives and a twenty-item test was used to increase precision) and both students and teachers were randomly assigned to tutoring and small class instruction (the teacher-to-student small-group ratios were 1:2 and 1:5). Classroom instruction involved a 1:23 ratio.

The results, again following thirty minutes of instruction, were:

1. Tutored students learned significantly more than students taught in groups of two, five, and twenty-three (defined as classroom instruction).
2. Students taught in both groups of two and five learned significantly more than those taught in the classroom.
3. There was no significant difference in learning between students taught in groups of two versus five (although a numerical difference favoring the former was observed).

The line graph in figure 5.1 rather dramatically illustrates these effects and underlines the learning potential for tutoring and very small-group instruction. (Note that the points between 5 and 23 were interpolated, not actually tested.)

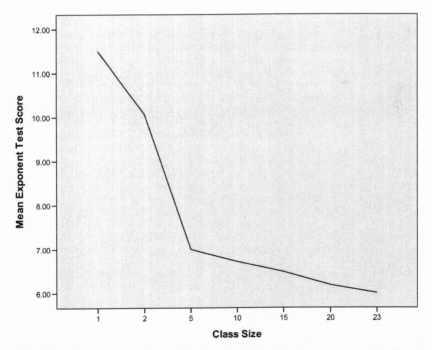

Figure 5.1 Learning Differences as a Function of Class Size. *Source*: Figure based upon interpolation of data in Moody, Bausell, & Jenkins (1973).

Implication: Admittedly going a bit away from the data, modeling the education system on the tutoring paradigm rather than the traditional classroom provides a far more promising avenue for the science. This is certainly the opinion of the central character of our next genre of research—to which the next chapter will be devoted.

Chapter 6

Research Genre #11: Programmatic Educational Research Conducted by a Single Investigator

Since science is created by scientists and one of the book's purposes is to explore why educational research hasn't resulted in any significant improvement in our schools, it would seem reasonable to examine the work of an exemplary individual scientist to see if any clues can be ascertained as to the cause of this failure.

While this approach may not merit a separate genre, one rationale for doing so revolves around two conflicting opinions among historians of science regarding how a science progresses. Namely, whether the greatest contributions thereto are determined by (a) day laborers who conscientiously contribute to building of their science's by laying a brick at a time to the overall edifice or (b) the occasional certifiable geniuses capable of making huge conceptual leaps that influence the choice of bricks for others to lay for decades (or centuries).

Certainly there is no question that education is a science that possesses no analogues to a Newton, Darwin, Pasteur, or Einstein. But this doesn't really serve as an excuse for education's lack of progress since even if these particular individuals had never been born, others in their disciplines would have made the same discoveries within a few years or decades. And while some potentially useful educational "discoveries" have been mentioned in the previous chapters, all would have been *obvious* to most of our *grandmothers*, which is a bit disconcerting.

So while the selected contributions of certain exemplary individual educational researchers (e.g., Edward Thorndike, Benjamin Bloom, and others) have been mentioned—all of whom would be excellent candidates for anyone's "all time" list of educational scientists—their contributions are now historic and any momentum they may have engendered in their time has long since dissipated. It therefore seemed that *perhaps* the examination of the cumulative work of a *single* extremely productive, respected, and *currently practicing* educational scientist might provide a hint regarding both the direction the discipline should take and the resources necessary for taking it.

The choice for the chosen candidate is based upon her programmatic endeavors, which primarily fit into Genre #10 (experiments conducted in schools under laboratory conditions) with her later work perhaps not perfectly fitting any of the previous nine.

This chapter is therefore designed to examine the work of this individual at what appears to be the zenith of her *ongoing* scientific career by (somewhat) systematically viewing it from the perspective of identifying any lessons her work might possess for improving the science of education. So after not a great deal of consideration, this investigator was chosen based upon her work's contribution to the *science of what could* be along with its:

1. Potential relevance to school learning;
2. Methodological soundness (i.e., the use of randomization, ensuring the fidelity with which her interventions are implemented, and a preference for curriculum-based rather than standardized tests);
3. Choice of instructional interventions (e.g., tutoring and additional instruction); and
4. Comfortable fit within the prescriptive curriculum → instruction → learning ≈ testing framework.

So now that the suspense has reached intolerable levels, it is time to announce the "winner": Lynn Fuchs of Vanderbilt University, who works with a team of researchers including her husband, Doug. It should be mentioned that the present author and Dr. Fuchs are not acquainted nor have ever corresponded with one another. Thus no claims can be made concerning inside information about the scientific intent or the genesis of her work other than her published record, her online resume, and an article about her in Vanderbilt University's newsletter.

A FEW FACTS ABOUT THE INVESTIGATOR

According to a brief biography on the Vanderbilt University website, Dr. Fuchs has published "over 350 empirical studies in peer-review journals" and the October 2015 version of her CV (available on the same website) ran eighty-eight pages. Her astonishing history of peer-reviewed publications began in 1981 (the same year she received her PhD) and has since been complemented by myriad awards, eighty-two listings under the topic "Chapters in Books, Booklets, Published Monographs, and Commissioned Papers," and according to an article in the *Vanderbilt Magazine*, she and her husband "have reportedly attracted more federal funding than any other researchers in their field."

This is not difficult to believe since by 2015 her CV listed fifty-three extramural research grants upon which she served as either principal investigator or project/director/codirector for a total of $71,907,325, and this doesn't count grants upon which she served in other capacities. (Altogether her CV listed seventy-one extramural awards for a mind-boggling total of $93,068,285.)

So, who could fail to be impressed by anyone who has garnered such a generous share of the nation's educational resources? And while a dollar-for-dollar comparison isn't possible, it is quite possible that the costs for development and evaluation of the Salk vaccine did not exceed $93,068,285 in present-day dollars. Still, despite your author's obvious selection acumen, a few disclaimers are in order before proceeding to address this chapter's aforementioned purposes.

First, no attempt was made to have read all 350+ peer reviewed articles written by Dr. Fuchs and her team or to claim that the ones selected for review were representative thereof. A good number of them were read, however, and the eleven selected here appeared to be among her largest projects *testing* the efficacy of instructional interventions designed to be *capable* of improving the learning of *at-risk* children in the early grades within the classroom setting.

Second, the proffered synopses were designed to be informative and to capture only the essence of the original experiments. They were originally presented via considerably more detailed descriptions of each experiment, but these were reduced since their total length would undoubtedly have consumed even the most conscientious readers' patience. Undoubtedly, in so doing many details were omitted that Dr. Fuchs and her coauthors considered important.

Third, while the work described will often be primarily singularly attributed to Dr. Fuchs for stylistic purposes, there is no way to separate any individual's work from the team within which he or she operates. Certainly her husband Doug, almost always a coauthor, contributes significantly to this awe-inspiring body of work. Otherwise her team's membership understandably changed over the decades represented here.

And finally, a number of idiosyncratic views are included editorially that are related to the purpose of *this* book (as viewed through the lens of our working hypothesis) that may be completely irrelevant (or even antithetical) to Dr. Fuchs's purposes for proposing and conducting the experiments in question. This is an important consideration to keep in mind since she would have (a) never heard of our working hypothesis (and surely would have dismissed it if she had) and (b) undoubtedly most likely did conduct her experiments for very different purposes than those for which this book is written.

Dr. Fuchs is, after all, very sincerely presented as an exemplary educational scientist and her career to this point is nothing short of astonishingly unparalleled. This, coupled with the methodological sophistication with which she designed and carried out her experiments is—after all—why her work was chosen to represent one investigator's (and team, as always) focused programmatic research agenda that has evolved over the most recent quarter of a century of the science's relatively young history.

From a methodological perspective, there is a great deal to like about her work, including the following six crucial principles relevant to the experimental assessment of learning efficacy to which Dr. Fuchs adheres in exemplary fashion:

1. Students or classrooms within schools are almost always *randomly assigned* to conditions to help ensure initial equivalence with respect to knowledge, prior educational experiences, and all other known and unknown variables.
2. The *fidelity* with which an instructional intervention is implemented (and monitored over the course of a study) is likewise always documented and jealously ensured when feasible.
3. The contents of the learning outcome measure and the *interventional* curriculum are typically congruent—which usually either requires investigators either to (a) construct their own learning measure rather than relying on standardized commercial tests or (b) construct their interventional curriculum to match an existing test.
4. The innovations tend to at least tangentially *modeled* on the tutoring paradigm. (The word "modeled" is emphasized because a controlled comparison between pure adult-delivered tutoring and classroom instruction is now utterly tautological.)
5. Sufficient preliminary pilot work appears to have always been performed prior to mounting a full-fledged trial.
6. The conduct of these trials appears to always be reported in an absolutely honest (and disarmingly transparent) fashion.

Now a few principles will be listed that Dr. Fuchs would not necessarily agree with (nor presumably would her peer review colleagues). Again, these principles are presented with the disclaimers that they don't necessarily apply to purely developmental work and (especially apparent in her later work) when her primary interest appears not to be the establishment of efficacy (which by then must have seemed almost tautological due to the repetitious nature of her interventions) to more "sophisticated" aspirations. (Again, the investigators "motivations" are completely speculative here.)

However, all eleven of these studies represent large educational random-ized controlled trials (RCTs) with at least some efficacy objectives and which report at least some efficacy conclusions—although her later work typically includes noncausal analyses as well. Therefore, with these disclaimers, the four *educational* research principles are:

1. Comparing an instructional innovation to a "business as usual" (i.e., regular classroom instruction) control/comparison group generally produces tautological results. Especially when the innovation's fidelity is carefully monitored, implemented, supervised, or supplemented by experimental staff who in turn are supervised by the investigators. This strategy provides an advantage to the intervention group(s) in com-parison to the control, which did not have access to these resources or anyone looking over the teachers' shoulders to ensure that a reasonable amount of relevant instruction was being delivered. Thus everything else being equal, the experiment *should* achieve statistical significance favoring an intervention group unless it is actually detrimental to learning.

2. If the intervention is more closely aligned with the learning outcome test than the comparison group, then everything else being equal the interven-tion group *should* perform significantly better on the outcome variable. And obviously if the intervention group teaches something that the com-parison group does not, then the former *should* perform significantly better on that *something* than the latter.

3. If the intervention group is provided with more instruction or more obvi-ously relevant instruction than the comparison group, then the intervention group *should* perform significantly better than the comparison group.

4. If a topic is taught and the outcome variable tests that topic from a *slightly* different perspective, then significant improvement on these items *should* occur anyway. True, most educational researchers would call this improvement *transfer of learning*, which, of course, they are free to do if they choose. But from this book's perspective, whenever something is taught in a competent, age-appropriate manner, some of that topic will be learned. And learning is learning regardless of what it is called.

In the present author's opinion, at least one of these principles, and often at least three, is/are often operative in the eleven experiments selected. And not coincidentally, all eleven reported at least some statistically significant results, which is essential to both publishing and grant procurement.

And while we are generally not concerned with research methodology here, the violation of these principles raises an important question:

Of what scientific benefit are experiments if their results are obvious?

However, the answer to this question may not be as "obvious" as it appears if some of this work provides non-efficacy-related findings important to the science or capable of informing future work that is. And (*spoiler alert*) some of these experiments make an impressive attempt at doing so.

The success or failure of these attempts on future endeavors is a matter of opinion, which is largely shaped by one's current perspective and vision of the future of the science. And by now you already know that the current author's opinions and perspectives are not shared by the most respected and successful educational scientists—of which Dr. Fuchs occupies a position at or very near the head of the class.

So, with these disclaimers in mind, why not sit back and enjoy reading what over $93 million can buy? Or, from another perspective, what can generate over $93 million in grant awards?

Study #1: An Early Peer-Tutoring Study (Fuchs et al. 1995). This was not the first experiment conducted by Dr. Fuchs, but with a body of work as large as hers, one has to begin somewhere. Her resume lists 125 published journal articles prior to this entry, and she had already received $3,347,983 in grant funding prior to the grant funding this study (which at $1,124,170 was the largest single award she had received to that point in her career). However, between this 1989 award and 1995 when this experiment appeared in print, Dr. Fuchs had received an additional seven research awards for a total of $2,084,658, and that doesn't include two grants whose funding she declined to accept (these totaled $672,099, which means that she's turned down more money than most educational researchers receive during their entire careers).

In other words, over two decades ago (when we begin to examine some of Dr. Fuchs's experimental work), she was already a mature professional whose career numbers were staggering. But let's ignore the number of publications, grants, and so forth and concentrate on the science.

This study was chosen because it appears to be relatively representative of the highly cited elementary-school-learning experiments involving learning-disabled students that she was to go on to publish in subsequent decades. As the title suggests, the intervention consisted of peer-mediated tutoring and was a refinement of an already venerable educational strategy that was apparently first implemented in India, then England in the early nineteenth century, and later in the United States, where it came to be called the Lancaster system, after Joseph Lancaster, one of its most influential proponents. These earlier strategies normally involved older students tutoring younger ones, the primary advantage of which were (a) economic (since the older tutors were not paid) and (b) instructional efficiency (since more instruction could be delivered within typically multiple-grade classrooms).

By 1977, enough research had been conducted on the process to inform a meta-analysis of twenty-nine studies involving mathematics achievement alone (Hartley 1977), and five years later, another such analysis was conducted employing fifty-two studies (Cohen, Kulik, and Kulik 1982).

Between 1995 and 2006, at least four additional meta-analyses were added on the topic, including a best-evidence synthesis by Dr. Fuchs herself (Mathes and Fuchs 1994), which incidentally is an excellent strategy to enable investigators to become thoroughly familiar with the literatures informing their work (not to mention garnering a publication). The bottom-line conclusion from these meta-analyses was that this mode of instruction resulted in increased learning for both the tutees and the tutors themselves, although perhaps less so for the latter. While not a fan of meta-analyses, these are mentioned as circumstantial evidence to support previous contentions:

1. That there is very little new under the educational research sun;
2. That we don't need redundant meta-analyses piled upon meta-analyses; and
3. That educational research is a very, very repetitive science.

It is important to note however, that a variation of the classic student-to-student tutoring model was tested in the Fuchs's studies reviewed here in the sense that the tutor–tutee role was rotated so that each member of the dyad both received and administered instruction. (This makes the procedure potentially more practical, since all students *receive* instruction.)

Also, instead of pulling students out of the classroom for experimental purposes, the Fuchs's approach involved all the students in a classroom simultaneously engaging in the process, which would make the model more practical as a schooling intervention. So, let's examine our first Fuchs study.

The investigators reported their motivation for conducting this peer-tutoring study was to extend previous research involving the venerable research strategy to ascertain if:

1. Students of different ability levels profited from the strategy;
2. It worked for math word problems as well as computation; and
3. The process affected teacher planning.

The experiment employed a design template that would characterize many of the team's later efforts, beginning with the recruitment of forty teachers instructing forty classrooms and randomly assigning teachers (along with their classrooms) to either implement peer-assisted tutoring or to continue with "business as usual," the latter condition serving as a control for the former.

Each teacher, experimental and control, was asked to identify a single student from her or his class to represent a different ability level (in this case, a low-achieving, average-achieving, and learning-disabled student; later a fourth, "above-average," student would be added). This particular study involved grades 2 and 4, with tutoring occurring twice per week for approximately thirty minutes for twenty-three weeks.

In addition, teachers collected weekly curriculum-based measurements (CBMs) that were scored by experimental staff. The results were used rather creatively to form tutor–tutee dyads in which the tutor was qualified to provide help and the tutee could benefit from said help.

The teachers were also required to fill out instructional-planning sheets that apparently were used as a fidelity check to help ensure (and document) teacher compliance with the experimental procedures. Another strategy probably designed for the same purpose involved unannounced periodic classroom observations of the experimental teachers by research assistants (RAs). The experimental teachers received training in the implementation of peer tutoring prior to the experiment and were assigned an RA consultant to be available throughout the course of the study.

The two primary outcomes for the study were (a) a computational test (called the acquisition measure) and (b) a transfer test consisting of word problems previously constructed by the first author and her colleagues based upon a systematic sampling of problems from the Tennessee elementary-school curriculum.

As would become a hallmark of a Fuchs study, the intervention effect was positive, indicating that overall the peer-mediated tutoring resulted in superior performance on the acquisition and transfer tests considered together. As would be expected, the effect size was larger for acquisition than transfer and there was no significant advantage for one "ability" level over another (called an aptitude-by-treatment interaction here).

Now certainly we could have predicted these results based upon our working hypothesis and the four experimental confounds stated above, but all in all this was a fine experiment, especially since one of the investigators' objectives appeared to be to use it to *construct* a viable classroom strategy capable of improving student learning.

Study #2: Peer-Assisted Instruction Involving Reading (Fuchs et al. 1997). Schools were randomly assigned this time (unusual for a Fuchs study) to treatment versus instruction-as-usual, thus producing a quasi-experimental design. The intervention consisted of partner reading of teacher-selected text (the stronger reader going first to facilitate the weaker reader's efforts), with activities designed to:

> provide students with intensive, systematic practice in reading aloud from narrative text, reviewing and sequencing information read, summarizing increasingly

large chunks of connected text, stating main ideas, and predicting and checking story outcomes. (Fuchs et al. 1997, 185)

The outcome variables were: (a) number of words read correctly, (b) number of comprehension questions answered correctly, and (c) number of maze words correctly supplied. The peer-assisted group scored significantly better on all three than the "business as usual" control. No differential learning effects was observed for the stronger versus the weaker readers, although of course the former outscored the latter. In their discussion section the authors transparently caution that:

> If a school district, for example, were to offer its teachers a 2-day in-service on PALS [peer-assisted learning] without follow-up, we would not expect the students of these teachers to achieve at a level comparable to that of the students in this study. (Fuchs et al. 1997, 199)

Study #3: Peer-"Mediated" Instruction Employing Conceptual Explanations (Fuchs et al. 1998).

As the title suggests, this study involved a refinement of the peer-tutoring process by extending math instruction from computation and simple problem-solving skills to conceptual instruction. The rationale for the study was based upon findings that cooperative learning is often characterized by (a) low-achieving students not participating satisfactorily in cooperative learning activities (O'Connor and Jenkins 1996) and (b) student tutors' tendencies in general to rely on lectures and demonstrations rather than teaching the tutees how to frame explanations or apply information (Fuchs et al. 1994).

Forty classrooms were randomly assigned to three groups: (a) ten classrooms to peer-mediated instruction along with training in "principles for offering and requesting elaborated help," (b) ten to the same peer-mediated instruction with training in elaborated help accompanied by instruction on providing "conceptual mathematical instruction," and (c) twenty to receive regular classroom instruction. An especially impressive aspect of the study was the explicit word-for-word scripts employed by the tutors (examples of which are presented as an appendix in the original article) that were prepared for the students to use in both the "generic" peer-mediated tutoring and (especially) the conceptual-mathematics explanation condition.

Outcome measures were computational and concepts/application tests designed by the team to reflect the "state's curriculum." One high-achieving, one medium-achieving, one low-achieving, and one learning-disabled student was selected from each class for data analytic purposes.

As always, the interventions were both significantly superior to the regular classroom instruction control for the operations and the concepts/applications outcomes, but the conceptual tutoring group also significantly outperformed its "nonconceptual" counterpart, which was somewhat surprising. However, since means and standard deviations were supplied, the present author personally contrasted the two subtests of the outcome variable (operations and concepts/applications) and found that the two interventions differed by (a) only one-half of an item on the computational subtest (which wasn't close to being statistically significant) but (b) by five items on the concepts/applications measure (*which was highly significant in favor of the group providing and receiving conceptual mathematical explanation*).

This is one more instance of the test being more closely aligned with one more experimental condition than the other and children learning what they are taught. Or conversely, it could be viewed an instance of children not being taught something also not learning it. But this in no way detracts from the uniqueness of the intervention itself (i.e., teaching children to teach conceptually).

The authors once again transparently warn that this intervention would most likely not translate to regular classroom instruction without the extra support provided to the teachers by the experimental staff.

Study #4: Peer-"Assistance" in Kindergarten (Fuchs, Fuchs, and Karns 2001).

Let's now skip ahead a few years and a few more million in grants with the Fuchs's still in the process of studying and developing the peer-assisted learning/instructional process. During this interval, Dr. Fuchs sandwiched in forty publications in peer-reviewed journals alone, at least five of which seemed to be developmental peer-assisted studies, apparently designed to guide her future work in the area. (Funding agencies are loath to approve studies that are not accompanied by pilot studies that both inform a proposed study and provide assurances that it will result in statistically significant results.) The five studies were:

1. A developmental study videotaping "10 high achievers working with both a high-achieving and with a low-achieving classmate on performance assessments."
2. A relatively small sample foray (also developmental or exploratory in nature) into assessing the effects of peer-assisted strategies on high school students with "serious reading problems."
3. A small-sample, developmental comparison of instruction as usual and peer-assisted collaborative reading activities, with and without elaborated help-giving.
4. A series of five pilot studies exploring methods of enhancing interactions during dyadic learning.
5. A randomized comparison of the collaborative effects of pairs of students versus small groups working on the completion of complex tasks as ascertained by the analysis of videos.

This 2001 study randomly assigned twenty classrooms to receive either peer-mediated or regular classroom instruction. The teachers in the experimental group (who were themselves trained and observed by grant paid RAs) trained their own students in the use of the instructional materials, with one student serving as the tutor/coach for half of the session before the roles were switched. High-, medium-, and low-achieving students were again employed, along with sixteen students with learning disabilities.

The procedures employed were very similar to previous studies (e.g., tutoring sessions were conducted twice weekly for twenty minutes over fifteen weeks) as were the results, which were positive for the peer-assisted condition on the mathematical-readiness test for all ability-level groups except the highest group (which performed significantly better than control on the Stanford test, as hypothesized). The investigators transparently reported that the tests employed were more closely aligned with the experimental curriculum by the investigators.

Unique aspects of the study were:

1. Suspecting the occurrence of a ceiling effect on the readiness test for the high ability students, a standardized achievement test was also employed upon which that group (but not the other ability levels) outperformed the business-as-usual control thereupon.
2. A subtle linguistic change in the title occurred in which the investigators reported they were enhancing mathematical *development* in kindergarteners. Certainly this is a nitpicking point, but development is a distal outcome in relationship to learning, and the effect of subtle language changes shouldn't be underestimated in selling the importance of a study to journal (and possibly) grant reviewers.
3. And, of course, successfully involving kindergarteners in the peer-assisted instructional process.

Study #5: Peer-"Assistance" in Enhancing First-Grade Mathematical Development (Fuchs et al. 2002)

This study might begin to sound familiar, but remember: ours is a *repetitive* science if nothing else. This time first-graders rather than kindergartners were employed along with a larger sample size. (Both were funded by the same grant [$3,515,150] and were supplemented via a large Vanderbilt Core Grant (which wasn't counted in Dr. Fuchs's total award numbers presented earlier since it didn't appear in her 2015 vitae [but was listed in an earlier version].)

Naturally the students having access to peer-assisted instruction performed better on the curriculum-aligned test than their randomly assigned controls, but no statistically significant differences surfaced on the nonaligned items.

The authors reported no statistically significant difference in the amount of math instruction administered between the experimental and control groups based upon weekly averages. However, according to the present author's calculations, despite the lack of statistical significance the average experimental student was the beneficiary of over nine hours of more mathematical instruction than the control group. (Should this calculation be incorrect, it should be attributed to your author's advanced age.)

Study #6: The Prevention, Identification, and Cognitive Determinants of Math Difficulty (Fuchs et al. 2005).

We now leap thirty-four journal articles ahead, many involving (a) developmental work and full-blown experiments investigating mathematical problem solving, (b) curriculum-based assessment, (c) reading fluency, and (d) a new construct (or at least a new term [i.e., math difficulty] for an old construct sometimes referred to as learning).

This study represents something of a departure for Dr. Fuchs in terms of language, interventions, and purpose:

1. With respect to language, she has now progressed from producing *learning* to fostering *development* and now to *prevention* (also quite distal to learning).
2. With respect to interventions, she has apparently left peer-mediated instruction behind and replaced it with small-group "tutoring" by *grant-paid*, well-educated, and supervised RAs.
3. And finally, with respect to intent, she has definitely moved beyond our simplistic four-component model of education (Curriculum → Instruction → Learning ≈ Testing) to one involving unseen processes within the brain.

For these and other reasons, this study is considerably more complicated than the previous five and can't really be done justice here. Even so, its description may exceed most readers' patience so apologies to readers are tendered in advance.

The design has also changed rather dramatically with 308 of the lowest-scoring students (plus eleven nominated by teachers) selected for additional individual testing. Of these, 139 students were classified as "at risk" candidates and then randomly assigned to receive either small-group instruction or an instruction-as-usual control group. (An additional, much larger "not at risk" group of students constituted a second, nonrandomized comparison group.)

Small-group instruction was performed in groups of two or three students by twelve well-educated RAs hired and trained by the investigators, and consisted of forty-eight sessions (thirty minutes each) taking place over a sixteen-week period. All small-group sessions were videotaped and, as would be expected, the intervention fidelity was extremely high since they were Fuchs employees.

Two sets of outcome variables were employed:

1. *Mathematical outcomes* that included (a) computation, (b) addition and subtraction fact retrieval, (c) concepts/applications (including numeration, geometry, measurement, graphs, and word problems), (d) the Woodcock Applied Problems test (including counting, telling time or temperature, and word problems), (e) story problems, and (f) curriculum-based measurements.

2. *Cognitive measures for correlational purposes* that included (a) intelligence (verbal, performance, and full-scale), (b) language (expressive vocabulary, verbal knowledge, and informational foundation) as well as verbal concept formation, abstract verbal-reasoning ability, and general intelligence, plus the ability to understand sentences and passages, (c) nonverbal problem solving and nonverbal fluid reasoning, (d) phonological processing (rapid digit naming and sound matching), (e) processing speed, (g) inductive ability (e.g., identifying objects that are different from a group of other objects plus the rule associated with the difference), (h) working memory, and (i) attention (as measured by a questionnaire filled out by the classroom teacher for each student).

Mathematical outcome results: To simplify matters, let's simply discuss the difference in improvement from pretest-posttest between the two randomized groups and leave the "not at risk" analyses for later. Basically, the very intensive small-group instructional intervention resulted in superior CBM assessments, the Woodcock calculations, the concepts/applications measure, and the story problems test. The intervention group did not exceed its control on either the addition or subtraction basic facts tests or the Woodcock applied-problems test.

The authors expressed some disappointment and surprise that the instructional program did not result in increased fact fluency (which the authors considered an important variable in contributing to math difficulty), but they nevertheless concluded that:

> Altogether, results do support the premise that first-grade tutoring can be effective in promoting stronger math outcomes, at least on three major aspects of performance: computation, concepts/applications, and story problems. (Fuchs et al. 2005, 507)

However, it would be very strange if all of this small-group instruction didn't improve *something*, but it is around this point in time (at least in the present author's opinion) that Dr. Fuchs begins to employ her model (part of which *requires* the production of a positive intervention effect) as a laboratory for searching for something less obvious than "more relevant instruction begets more learning." (*Spoiler alert*: not to spoil the story's ending, but remember this is an *obvious* science.)

Prevalence and severity of math difficulty: The construct the authors designated as math difficulty will become an important component of their future work, so we will need to discuss it in a bit more detail. The investigators noted that there are myriad ways to define math difficulty that provide different prevalence estimates. They consequently employed *sixteen* methods of measuring the construct.

Basically these myriad assessments involve testing different components of prior mathematical learning emanating from school (and the home instructional environment, don't forget) and then devising a variety of cut points within the continuum or combination of scores to separate students who (a) *have* "difficulty" with math versus (b) those who *do not*. In other words, students labeled as having *math difficulty* have learned less mathematics than children who are not so labeled.

Across the myriad different methods of measuring the math difficulty construct (not counting three different ways of using the CBM results, which were almost perfectly aligned with the small-group instructional curriculum) there were an average of four out of sixty-four fewer intervention students with math difficulty at the end of the school year than their sixty-three control counterparts. Hardly surprising, since we already know that students subject to interventions involving small-group instruction more closely aligned to the tests *perform* better on those tests than their control counterparts who are not taught the tests.

While admitting that math difficulty was a "soft" disability with no physical markers, the authors concluded that "across the 16 methods for which figures could be computed, tutoring resulted in a mean 35.64% reduction" of the disability. *Recall that this figure represented a grand total difference of four students*. (The most impressive of the sixteen different analyses resulted in a reduction in math difficulty of 40.11 percent involving an actual difference of *two students* identified with math difficulty in the randomly assigned control group versus none in the intervention group.)

The authors then provide estimates of the number of children who would be affected if their intervention were to be implemented nationwide. *Somewhat* of a stretch since it was based upon a four-student difference between two experimental conditions, which of course did not approach statistical significance.

Relationships between the math outcomes and the cognitive variables: The final study purpose involved exploring "the cognitive abilities associated with the development of mathematics competence in first grade." Statistically, this was accomplished by assessing the relationship between each of the five mathematics outcomes and the seven cognitive variables employing all three groups of students: (a) the "at risk" intervention group, (b) the "at risk" group control group, and (c) the nonrandomized "not at risk" comparison group.

A somewhat worrisome component of this analysis is that the authors *statistically* controlled the differences among these groups via multiple regression procedures (which could be conceptualized as an extension of our *Bogus Assessment Principle #2*, but this time assuming that algebra can make "at risk" students equivalent to "not at risk" ones). R-E-A-L-L-L-Y?

Each analysis was repeated multiple times in order to isolate the unique percentage of variation among individual students' math outcomes that could be "explained" by the cognitive measures employed. Basically, the most consistent unique predictor of end-of-year performance for each dependent variable was found to be the teachers' ratings on a four-item scale of their students' "attention." This proved to be a unique predictor of all five outcomes with an average explained amount of students' individual differences being a less than overwhelming 2.4 percent. The next most predictive cognitive variable was "phonological processing," which was significantly predictive of three of the five outcomes and explained an even more underwhelming 1.4 percent of the students' differences in test scores.

And despite the authors' assurance that contributions to individual differences in math performance in the 2 percent range "are not trivial," many researchers (including *your* curmudgeon author) would consider them so. And even if the 2.4 percent "predictive ability" afforded by the teachers' ratings of "attention" isn't trivial, it may well have been influenced by teacher knowledge of the student's past achievement (ergo even this small proportion of variance obtained may have been tautological).

Also, when encountering impressive-sounding assessments (such as verbal concept formation, nonverbal fluid reasoning, phonological processing, processing speed, inductive ability, and so forth) it wouldn't hurt to keep *Bogus Assessment Principle #4* in mind:

Just because somebody writes some items to measure something and gives it that thing's name doesn't mean (a) that the resulting instrument measures what its developers think it measures or (b) that the targeted construct even exists.

Implications: So was this study worth conducting? Perhaps it was. After all, we have the benefit of hindsight here and the Fuchs team can't be criticized for not being aware of either our bogus assessment principles or our working hypothesis (and undoubtedly wouldn't agree with them anyway). But going forward rather than looking backward, from the perspective of *this* book, and the *working hypothesis* guiding it, *nothing much is likely to be accomplished from future studies such as this and certainly nothing has been accomplished so far that could benefit students.* However, this is only one person's opinion and probably a minority one at that, so let's continue.

Study #7: Effects of Small-Group Tutoring with and without Validated Classroom Instruction on At-Risk Students' Math Problem Solving: Are Two Tiers of Prevention Better Than One? (Fuchs et al. 2008).

Skipping a few dozen more publications (including full-scale randomized trial reports, some continuing the search for cognitive correlates of math difficulty, and at least eight articles advocating the advantages of the response to intervention [RTI] approach), the following 2008 study was selected because it represents a tantalizing hint of a very, very innovative instructional environment.

But first, let's consider the *"response to intervention"* concept, which involves giving a name to a common-sense educational approach involving identifying and remediating instructional problems. The initial step in the process involves screening students on basic math and/or reading topics that they should know at their particular grade level. Those children who perform below expectations are then monitored via frequently administered CBMs with each child's performance graphed over time. If he or she does not appear to be improving at an acceptable rate, then a second, more-intensive "tier" (another new term for an old concept) of instruction is delivered, which most commonly consists of tutoring or small-group instruction.

The method of instruction chosen for the intervention in this study is known as schema-based problem solving which, believe it or not, is yet another (but not new) term for a common-sense instructional approach. It is based upon the fact that practically all math problems differ from one another in *some* way, but often share some commonalities as well. Students are therefore taught techniques to identify and understand commonalities among problems as well as how to solve those problems containing common elements. This strategy had been independently and definitively demonstrated to result in improved problem-solving performance by a sizable number of investigators in different settings, hence the "validated classroom instruction" moniker in the study's title.

One hundred and twenty third-grade classrooms were randomly assigned to receive (a) thirteen weeks of conventional problem-solving instruction from their regular classroom teachers (i.e., "business as usual") or (b) thirteen weeks of instructor-designed schema-broadening instruction (SBI) from RAs trained, employed, and supervised by the study investigators. Prior to this thirteen-weeks instructional interval, the RAs delivered three weeks of general math problem-solving instruction designed by the research team to both conditions in all 120 classrooms. (Note that Dr. Fuchs seems to have [understandably] completely given up reliance on classroom teachers to deliver any of the experimental instruction—classroom or small group.)

All conventional and intervention (SBI) students were carefully screened to identify students who were "at risk" for poor problem-solving achievement. This resulted in 243 "at risk" students who were eligible for tutoring and 878 "not at risk" students who were not tutored but who were randomized either to receive or not receive SBI instruction.

The 243 "at risk" students were then randomly assigned within each of the other two groups (i.e., classrooms receiving convention delivered by regular classroom instructors versus those receiving SBI classroom instruction from RAs) to either receive or not receive small-group instruction (involving two to four students). None of the "not at risk" students received tutoring so obviously were not randomized to this second tier of instruction.

Considering only the "at risk" students, this strategy produced a 2 (conventional versus SBI classroom instruction) × 2 (small-group instruction versus no small-group instruction) factorial design comprised of four different experimental scenarios:

1. Those receiving conventional problem-solving instruction but no small-group instruction,
2. Those receiving SBI classroom instruction but also no small-group instruction,
3. Those receiving conventional problem solving instruction and small-group instruction, and
4. Those receiving SBI classroom instruction and small-group instruction.

This is a very strong design as it permits two interventions to be compared in the same experiment separately as well as testing the possibility that they have a *cumulative effect* with respect to one another (something all-too-rarely investigated in education). And in this case, such an effect was observed as depicted by the following results (which the present author took the liberty of gleaning from one of the investigators' other tables).

What this table clearly indicates is that the SBI instruction was superior to conventional (i.e., business-as-usual) classroom instruction (31.58 versus 17.53) and that small-group instruction was superior to no small-group instruction (31.46 versus 17.65). Even more importantly, small-group instruction combined with SBI classroom instruction was significantly superior to all four of the other cells (39.06 versus 24.09, 23.86, and 11.20).

From a policy perspective, however, this may be the most important finding in any of the studies reviewed here. True, it may be obvious given that:

Table 6.1   2 x 2 Factorial Results

	Small-Group Instruction	No Small-Group Instruction	Classroom Instruction with and without Small-Group Instruction
Monitored SBI Classroom Instruction Delivered by Trained RAs	39.06	24.09	31.58
Unmonitored Conventional Instruction Delivered by Teachers Not Trained in SBI	23.86	11.20	17.53
Small-Group Instruction with and without Small-Group Instruction	31.46	17.65	

1. The SBI classroom instruction versus the non-SBI classroom instruction was confounded by the fact that the RA teachers were monitored by their employers and the classroom teachers were basically free to do their "own thing," hence undoubtedly the former squeezed in more actual problem-solving instruction than the latter;
2. The small-group instruction in this study involved both additional *time* (it was administered in addition to the regular mathematics instruction) and *relevance* (since it simulates the tutoring paradigm and its content mirrored the SBI model); and
3. The only conceivable reason why the two interventions shouldn't be cumulative (i.e., additive) is if the SBI classroom instruction and the small-group instruction were redundant with one another.

However, this is a *breakthrough* in the development of a controlled educational research laboratory located within a traditional school that has policy implications far beyond the laboratory. In other words (and perhaps attempting to cross *several* bridges too far beyond the data), what this study illustrates is that classroom instruction can be made considerably more *relevant* if teachers are prescriptively trained to deliver the curriculum in such a way that it maximally matches the outcome variable and *then* are supervised to ensure that they do. (Both specific curricular training and close supervision are crucial and neither is present with this degree of intensity in the public schools.)

Now, of course, this latter finding (or perhaps more correctly, this implication) will probably never inform actual school practice so it rests solidly in the realm of the *science of what could be* rather than *what is* or *what will be*. And even if the remainder of the study boils down to a methodologically sophisticated, skillful, and scholastic illustration of the *obvious*, the bottom line is that *better studies than this just aren't being conducted in education.* And for what little it's worth, the experimental component of this study ranks among the present author's favorites and he would place it among the top ten educational research experiments of all time.

The study's nonexperimental component: As always not knowing for sure, Dr. Fuchs's personal agenda at the time may have been more ambitious that either the randomized effects or the laboratory model just discussed. Instead, she may have set her sights upon addressing one of the most important scientific and clinical issues in education. An issue important enough to transcend the existence of the study's experimental confounds (of which Dr. Fuchs and her team were certainly aware) or the results' obviousness. Namely, whether *the persistent, omnipresent learning gap for students "at risk" for a poor learning prognosis could be reduced in comparison with students with more propitious educational prognoses.*

The investigators declared success here because the "at risk" students who received both experimental conditions did gain more from pretest to posttest than the "not at risk" students. However, in the present author's opinion (and this is *only* an opinion) this may also be going a bridge too far even if the effort itself should be applauded.

The problems with the investigators' approach are seen to be the following:

First, if (a) a large preexisting learning gap exists between two groups of students (e.g., one with lower test scores on a specific topic than the other) and if (b) the group with the lower scores is intensively taught the contents of the test longer than and more intensively than the other—then isn't it rather obvious that the "learning gap" will be *reduced*? (Or, on the other side of this coin, if two groups started out equally on the test and one was taught the subject matter informing the test long enough and the other was not, wouldn't a "learning gap" be *created*?)

So the objection here is there are different types of learning gaps. One is situationally and subject-matter specific that can be addressed by a *relatively* short-term but intensive intervention specific to the subject matter. This study addressed the former and not the latter, so—as in Study #6, the use of the word "prevention" in the title is problematic (i.e., *Effects of Small-Group Tutoring with and without Validated Classroom Instruction on At-Risk Students' Math Problem Solving: Are Two Tiers of Prevention Better Than One?*).

Certainly more instruction (two tiers) is better than less (one tier), but nothing is being prevented *here* as far as we know. What we are dealing with here is "only" relatively short-term learning. Assessments of long-term learning gains are rare, but Jenkins et al. (2006) followed a group of learning-disabled and special-education children from preschool (where they were randomized to contrasting preschool curricula, one of which proved to be more effective than the other) to nineteen years of age and found that graduates of both curricula still functioned at around one standard deviation below the average student in terms of achievement despite additional special education "interventions" during the intervening years.

Forgetting semantics, however, another problem that exists with the Fuchs strategy involves the incomparability of the "not at risk" and "at risk" groups with respect to pretest knowledge of the curriculum. The crux of this comparison involves ascertaining if the learning gap was decreased involving pre-posttest *gains*, which in turn involves comparing students with high pretest scores (i.e., "not at risk") versus students with low pretest scores (i.e., "at risk"). Everything being equal, there are several reasons why it is easier to achieve greater gains from students with low pretest scores than those with high pretest scores *in addition to* the fact that the former received a substantial amount of relevant tutoring and the latter did not.

One is regression to the mean. Another is the fact that more difficult concepts require more instructional time to learn than easier concepts and the "not at risk" students probably answered more of the easier pretest items correctly than the more difficult pretest items. Hence they would naturally require more instructional time to master the latter but in effect they received less instruction than their "at risk" counterparts. And finally, since the "not at risk" group contained some "at risk" students (at least as measured by the authors' cherished "math difficulty" construction), this would itself serve to slightly reduce the "true" gap between the two groups (both prior to and especially following instruction).

Yet despite all of these objections, the "not at risk" students receiving the SBI curriculum had numerically higher posttest scores than the "at risk" SBI students. So the "gap" may have been closed a bit by the extra instruction, but in the final analysis the "not at risk" students retained their superiority even following this intensive dose of instruction in a specific curricular topic. And even if something was "prevented," we'll never know what it was.

Implications: In effect, what this study demonstrates is that children learn more when they receive more relevant instruction (i.e., SBI) and greater amounts of it (i.e., SBI small-group instruction). Therefore the question that many teachers (if any had the patience to read this complex study) and policy-oriented individuals would have is "*So what?*"

So what if both Groups "A" and "B" are given instruction in a topic and "B" students (think "not at risk") perform better because they had been the recipients of additional instruction in the past (either on the topic or on related material)? Isn't it *obvious* that if we kept teaching and tutoring everyone in group "A" ("at risk" who received less prior instruction) that they would *eventually* score as highly as group "B" (which they did *not* in this particular study)? At least if there was enough time in the school day?

Now, of course, both aspects of the study (the 2 × 2 design and the "at risk" versus "not at risk" analysis) can be defended on the basis that they are illustrations of the science of what "could be" rather than "what is." But regardless of how anyone conceptualizes this study's results, the investigators deserve kudos for performing an experimental rarity: *the assessment (even if it is an obvious one) of the cumulative effects of two effective interventions, which should be a far more common research goal in educational research than it is*—especially since so many educational interventions are potentially cumulative and the process of educating children is a cumulative endeavor.

Study #8: Remediating Number Combinations and Word Problem Deficits among Students with Mathematics Difficulties: A Randomized Control Trial (Fuchs et al. 2009).

This time, the following three groups of third-graders were employed who were identified as having both reading and math difficulty, with extremely low IQ scores being excluded from the latter group:

1. Tutoring based upon automatic retrieval of *number combinations* (basically simple addition and subtraction) using a counting strategy (when needed) and computerized practice accompanied by reinforcement (the possibility of winning small prizes based upon the number of gold stars obtained).
2. Tutoring on solving *word problems* that included (a) the counting strategy for addition and subtraction, (b) review of double-digit addition and subtraction, (c) "conceptual and strategic" word-problem instruction *including prealgebraic content*, (d) review, and (e) the same reinforcement strategy as the first group.
3. A no-tutoring control.

Third-grade students were screened in order to identify those with (a) math difficulty only or (b) both math difficulty and reading difficulty (the twenty-sixth percentile was used as the cut point for both math and reading, although the latter group also excluded individuals with extremely low IQ scores). Students were then randomly assigned to the three groups. (The two experimental groups received the usual classroom instruction plus three twenty- to thirty-minute tutorial sessions per week as described above for sixteen weeks while the control students received regular classroom instruction.)

So we know how this one came out. Both tutored groups outperformed the control; students that were taught to solve word problems did better than those who were taught computation; those who were identified with only one learning deficiency (math difficulty) did better on word problems than those who had dual math and reading difficulties.

Study #9: Effects of First-Grade Number Knowledge Tutoring with Contrasting Forms of Practice (Fuchs et al. 2013).

This study continued Dr. Fuchs's work on efficient counting procedures for low-achieving students (designed to mitigate difficulties with the memorization of basic math facts). It also continued her new propensity (beginning with Study #6) to use a rather straightforward experiment (which produces obvious causal learning results) to generate noncausal correlational work that hopefully would delve into unobservable effects presumably occurring somewhere within the brain.

So let's consider the experiment first. Here, thirty minutes of one-to-one tutoring was employed for "at risk" first-graders three times a week for sixteen weeks. (Sound familiar?) Students were randomly assigned to three groups: two that received different forms of short-term practice tacked on to the end of each tutoring session and one group that received no tutoring at all. The curriculum and instructional procedures for the two tutored conditions were identical for the first twenty-five minutes of each session with the final five minutes differing as follows:

1. *Nonspeeded practice* "designed to reinforce the relations and principles that serve as the basis of reasoning strategies that support fact retrieval. Operationally it consisted of students playing games with space-theme manipulatives "designed to provide contextualized review of the content addressed in the day's lesson" (Fuchs et al. 2013, 63).
2. *Speeded practice* "designed to promote quick responding and the use of efficient counting procedures to generate many correct responses and thereby form long-term representations to support retrieval" (Fuchs et al. 2013, 59). Operationalized, this involved quickly supplying the answers to flash-card-contained problems and using counting procedures when the answers were not immediately known.

Naturally, both tutoring conditions outperformed the none-tutored students on all four of the math outcomes employed (simple arithmetic, complex calculations [basic operations involving two-digit numbers], number knowledge, and orally read word problems). The speeded tutored group outperformed the nonspeeded tutored group on simple arithmetic and two-digit calculations but not on number knowledge or orally read word problems.

Both sets of findings were painfully obvious and anyone who doesn't know that tutoring is better than no tutoring by now is "at risk" for a lot more than math difficulty. Or that the forty-eight, five-minute speeded practice sessions devoted to learning simple arithmetic facts plus two-digit calculations might just result in superior test performance on simple arithmetic facts and two-digit calculations than the group who spent their time playing games and manipulating space ships.

However, similar to Experiment #7 (the "two-tiers of prevention" study), a second correlational study accompanied the experimental design employing a plethora of cognitive variables—this time to identify potential aptitude-by-treatment interactions (which will shortly be award the distinction of our fourth Education Urban Legend and is defined as interventions that are significantly more effective for some types of students than other [or even that are effective for some and detrimental for others, which is called a disordinal aptitude-by-treatment interaction].)

Aptitude-by-treatment interactions: as elusive as Bigfoot, for the same reason. One objective that seemed to be in the process of becoming a quixotic search for Dr. Fuchs at this point was to tease out an aptitude-by-treatment interaction hidden somewhere within the relationships between the plethora of cognitive variables she had begun to employ (in this case seven) and mathematical outcomes (this time simple arithmetic and word problems, each of which possessed a pretest). (It is unclear why the number knowledge and complex-calculation outcomes were not employed, perhaps because as the number of tests performed increases so is the likelihood of obtaining false positive results.)

In any event, fourteen potential aptitude-by-treatment interactions were computed involving (a) the two math outcomes and (b) each separate cognitive variable divided into low, medium, and high scores (based upon standard deviations) combined with the four study groups (the two types of tutoring, the nontutored "at risk" students, *and* the "not at risk" comparison group).

This model is somewhat troublesome for sticklers such as the present author because of the inclusion of the "not at risk" students, whose pretest scores would be expected to be significantly higher than that of the other three groups and therefore not comparable even when this discrepancy is statistically controlled. But anyway, the *Cliffs Notes* version of these analyses is that three statistically significant interactions were obtained between both the experimental conditions/groups and the nonexperimental "not at risk" group. However, only one of these analyses (involving simple computation as the "aptitude" and nonverbal reasoning as the "attribute" approximated anything resembling an aptitude-by-treatment interaction for the three randomly assigned groups involving "at risk" students, so let's examine that one with the "not at risk" deleted since it simply muddies the water here.

Interactions are most easily interpreted when they are graphed because differences in the slopes (or lines) indicate what the interaction is comprised of. Parallel lines indicate the absence of an interaction; nonparallel lines (when accompanied by a significant *p*-value) indicate the presence of an interaction via a graphic depiction of which group differs from which other group. So let's examine the present author's less-than-professional representation of the original article's Figure 2, Panel A (sans the "not at risk" group since it didn't appear to contribute to the interaction):

Now obviously these three lines are not parallel with one another, so assuming that this configuration remains statistically significant without the contribution of the "not-at-risk" data (which it may well not, because all of the groups' adjusted scores [hence their slopes] depicted in this figure are influenced by the "not-at-risk" group's scores), the practical or clinical implications of this interaction are unimpressive.

First, we already know that the speeded intervention (represented by the top line) was superior to both the nonspeeded and the control conditions on this outcome (simple addition and subtraction computation). This is clearly reflected by comparing the top line to the bottom two lines at both –1SDs (the left-most points) and +1SDs (those on the right). And while the speeded intervention outperformed the nonspeeded intervention at all levels of the nonverbal reasoning continuum (shown by the difference between the top two

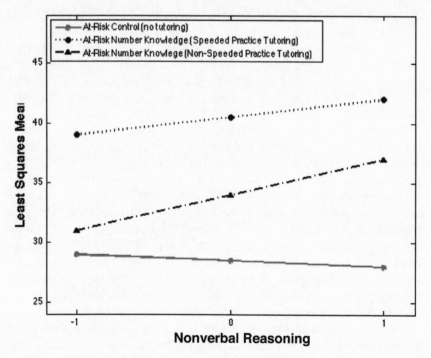

Figure 6.1   Reconfigured Aptitude × Treatment Interaction.

lines), the difference was considerably greater at the lower end (i.e., left most point) of the continuous attribute than the higher end (the right most point).

Whether this difference is statistically significant or not when the basically artefactual "not-at-risk" scores are deleted can't be ascertained from the information presented. Regardless, however, this difference doesn't seem to be all that important since we can see (and know from the results) that the speeded intervention is superior to its nonspeeded counterpart and both are superior to the no-tutoring group. Thus the clinical implications seem obvious (since both interventions appear to consume the same amount of resources):

Regardless of a student's nonverbal reasoning level, use the speeded tutoring intervention and forget the nonspeeded intervention. (And forget nonverbal reasoning level as well.)

However, from an efficacy point of view, we need to consider the control group in our deliberations. Here the difference between the two interventions and control is quite striking. The nonspeeded intervention doesn't seem dramatically more efficacious than the control at very low levels of nonverbal reasoning although it is *numerically* superior. However, it does appear to be relatively more efficacious in comparison to control for higher levels of nonverbal reasoning (and of course the difference between the speeded intervention and control at that end is even greater). So *now* the clinical implications are:

Regardless of a student's nonverbal reasoning level, use the speeded tutoring intervention and forget the nonspeeded intervention. (So again, forget nonverbal reasoning as well.)

Now no one would call this finding particularly obvious, and certainly most of our grandmothers would experience difficulty interpreting all of this. (And none would have had the patience to have read this far into this synopsis, but they wouldn't have much trouble with the bottom-line conclusion that if Method A is always better than Method B but never worse, then, everything else being equal we should go with Method A.) And that pretty much sums up the practical implications of most ordinal aptitude-by-treatment interactions when they do occur, which they rarely do.

Needless to say, this interpretation of these results probably doesn't mirror that of the investigators. However, from this perspective this is an extremely expensive experiment that found that children who receive more instruction relevant to certain outcomes learn more of those outcomes than those who receive less instruction.

To be fair, however, Dr. Fuchs did find (here and previously) that expending huge amounts of time in teaching children who find it difficult to memorize basic arithmetic facts may squander time that could be devoted to more useful content—hence her advocacy of teaching more-efficient, simple counting techniques. Of course, even those approaches might not be necessary for children in this digital age where electronic calculators are present everywhere including cell phones.

The investigators also probably shouldn't be criticized for at least attempting to glean the inner workings of the brain to figure out the etiology of why some interventions are effective and others are not—especially since they aren't privy to our simplistic working hypothesis or Bogus Assessment Principle #4. Surely investigators this prolific should occasionally attempt to see just how far their reach extends, even if the result is grasping a handful of air.

Also, few modern investigators spend a great deal of time studying the past of their science, which long ago produced the rationale for the promised fourth and final urban legend (to which Dr. Fuchs most certainly would not subscribe):

Education Urban Legend #4: Some Instructional Methods Are More Effective for Some Students and Actually Harmful for Others

An Aside Illustrating That Even in the Science of the Obvious, Everything That's Obvious Isn't Necessarily True

Historically, the absence of research pointing to the superiority of any instructional methods over any others when time and the curriculum were controlled was counterintuitive to many educators. There just had to be some instructional methods besides tutoring that would dramatically increase student learning in the schools as compared to a teacher simply standing in front of a class and teaching!

Nowhere is this better illustrated than in the case of an eminent educational psychologist named Lee J. Cronbach (1957), who gave a stirring call-to-arms on the topic in his inaugural presidential address to the American Psychological Association. Professor Cronbach advanced a deceptively simple (and intuitively attractive) hypothesis for explaining why nothing seemed to work better than anything else in the classroom. (History does not record whether he was an adherent of the excrement principle, but the chances are he wasn't.)

Borrowing from the concept that different students have different learning styles, Professor Cronbach suggested that it was the ubiquitous presence and potency of these differences that explained why no one could find any learning differences attributable to instructional methods when time and teacher effects were controlled. (Tutoring and class size being an exception.)

He consequently suggested that in a research study contrasting a new, well-conceived innovation such as Innovative Instructional Method A with Instructional Method B, students would exist in most classroom settings who would be differentially affected by the two methods. Thus, students who possessed high amounts of Attribute X (whatever that "X" happened to be) might benefit from New Method A, but would actually learn less when taught by Method B.

To make life a bit more difficult for educational researchers, however, there might well be another cadre of students who possessed Attribute Y (or were low on Attribute X) for whom the opposite would be true. Obviously then, when two instructional methods were contrasted with one another in the same research study, the differential learning resulting from the two types of students (or perhaps there were myriad such attributes in play) would tend to largely cancel each other out, thereby disguising the fact that there really were important differences between the two methods for different types of students. This very hypothetical scenario is illustrated in the following table 6.2, which if graphed would result in two crossing lines approximating the letter "X."

Professor Cronbach consequently suggested that researchers needed to increase their efforts to investigate these "aptitude-by-treatment interactions." This generated considerable interest and enthusiasm among educational researchers, because it potentially explained the frustrating failure of the discipline to produce findings with any useful practice or policy implications. However, despite the hypothesis's intuitive appeal, it had one small problem. No one had ever observed the damned things.

To make matters worse, an extensive review of the literature conducted a decade or so after the great man's clarion call basically concluded that the techniques for identifying these effects were "often an afterthought rather than a carefully planned part of the experiment" and that "this approach has not been successful in finding meaningful disordinal interactions" (Bracht 1970, 639).

Said another way, these "dueling aptitudes" simply did not appear to be causal factors in the failure to document the superiority of an instructional method when instructional time and the fidelity to the experimental curriculum were controlled. And, alas, little occurring over the ensuing decades has changed this basic conclusion; although the basic concept retains a degree of

Table 6.2 A Perfectly Disordinal Aptitude X Treatment Interaction with the Cells Representing Hypothetical Mean Learning Scores

	High Aptitude X	Low Aptitude X	Total
Method A	60.0	40.0	50.0
Method B	40.0	60.0	50.0
Total	50.0	50.0	

popularity, since even useless constructs and theories that disappear from the literature are often reborn again a few decades later.

A somewhat sad endnote to this little episode occurred when Cronbach himself later acknowledged researchers' failure to find his cherished interactions, but, undaunted, suggested the abandonment of statistics and science in favor of "intensive local observation" since "too narrow an identification with science . . . has fixed our eyes upon an inappropriate goal" (Cronbach 1975).

Study #10: Does Working Memory Moderate the Effects of Fraction Intervention? An Aptitude-by-Treatment Interaction (Fuchs et al. 2014b)—or déjà vu all over again.

This study represents a continuation of Dr. Fuchs's search for a meaningful aptitude-by-treatment interaction. Otherwise this study is quite similar to several other past efforts in the sense that:

1. The usual plethora of psychological measures were employed to investigate what is *really* going on that can explain why some children learn less,
2. Two forms of five-minute practice sessions were added to the end of multiweek, thirty-minute tutoring sessions,
3. A business-as-usual control was employed, and of course
4. The search for aptitude-by-treatment interactions continued unabated.

As usual, both interventions produced significantly greater learning gains than control—this time for the three fraction-related outcomes employed, although the two interventions did not differ significantly from one another on any of the three outcomes.

The investigators then went on to test an aptitude-by-treatment interaction involving one of their psychological measures (working memory) and two interventions (conceptual versus fluency practice) with respect to the fractions number line outcome. The specific effect hypothesized was that students with poor working memory would profit more from the fluency than the conceptual practice conditions.

Using an *exploratory* procedure developed by Johnson and Neyman (1936) to ascertain the *location* within the aptitude's score *continuum* a significant interaction occurs (a strategy that definitely capitalizes on chance if the location is not hypothesized a priori), the investigators found one that occurred only *below the tenth percentile of at-risk students on listening recall* (the subtest the authors used to represent the working-memory battery).

Now if anything, this interaction had even less clinical application than the one identified in Study #9 because a typical classroom would be unlikely to have more than a single student falling below the tenth percentile on this variable. However, one of the most appealing aspects of a Fuchs study is her transparency in reporting her results as represented by the following quote:

caution in interpreting this effect is warranted because results did not corrobo-
rate the fluency practice compensation hypothesis, as indicted in Fuchs, Geary,
et al. [2013]). (Fuchs et al. 2014b, 510)

Both the practical and scientific importance of the interaction is also
reduced by the fact that the analysis controlled for attentive behavior and
"processing speed" *in addition to* their moderating effects, hence it is difficult
to conceptualize the exact meaning of the resulting adjusted fraction number
line score. The authors also (again) transparently affix the following episte-
mological warning label:

> We also remind readers that such moderation analyses are correlational, so as
> with the mediation analyses, inferences about causation should be applied with
> caution. Also, although this study's dramatic illustration of an aptitude–treat-
> ment interaction suggests the need to personalize intervention, corroborating
> studies are required. (Fuchs et al. 2014b, 511)

Well, to call this a "dramatic illustration" when it involves only students
below the tenth percentile on a questionable psychological construct may be
somewhat of a stretch, but probably if your author had conducted this study
he would have found it dramatic as well: perhaps even *traumatic*, since it
did not occur in the hypothesized direction. And on the basis of this nonhypothesized finding, the authors' clarion call for more research on aptitude-
by-treatment interactions (reminiscent of Lee J. Cronbach's over half of a
century earlier) may be even more of a stretch:

> Even so, present results—when combined with accumulating evidence that the
> effects of intervention depend on individual differences in cognitive abilities
> or prior domain knowledge—indicate the importance of considering aptitude–
> treatment interactions in future studies. Intervention design for AR students and
> those with reading or mathematics learning disabilities has improved substan-
> tially over past decades. . . . Aptitude–treatment interactions provide a paradigm
> that may eventually provide the basis for personalizing intervention in ways that
> expand efficacy. (Fuchs et al. 2014b, 512)

Has the repetitive nature of our science or its complete lack of "working
memory" been mentioned? Or Glenn Bracht's (1970) analysis of the fruits
of Professor Cronbach's contention that aptitude-by-treatment interactions
were the future of instructional research? Or Bracht's conclusion that these
interactions are rare, almost never replicate, and that disordinal aptitude-by-
treatment interactions that occur as *hypothesized* are practically nonexistent
(recall that the one reported in this study occurred in a nonhypothesized,
unexpected direction).

Study #11: Does Calculation or Word Problem Instruction Provide a Stronger Route to Prealgebraic Knowledge? (Fuchs et al. 2014a).

This one involved similar procedures to those used in Study #7 (but given the collective memory of the profession, no one would have remembered this if the authors hadn't cited it). Specifically, it involved the two-tiered approach and both classroom instruction and small-group instruction tiers delivered by trained, supervised RAs. However, this time the instruction-as-usual control was delivered by trained RAs (although sans any small-group instruction).

Second-grade students were screened from 127 classrooms taught by ninety-six teachers in order to classify students who were (a) low on calculation and word-problem achievement, (b) low on one of the two, or (c) not low on either. (Perhaps reminiscent of a previous study involving students low on math, low on reading, and low on both but when you conduct this many studies a little recycling is inevitable). Classrooms were then randomly assigned to conditions, the two intervention groups being:

1. The calculation intervention consisted of two forty- to forty-five-minute classroom sessions per week for seventeen weeks delivered by an RA and accompanied by thirty-nine small-group sessions of twenty-five to thirty minutes each (also delivered by an RA). This curriculum emphasized (a) "interconnected knowledge about number" and (b) practice solving one- and two-digit problems using both memory and counting procedures.
2. The word-problem intervention involved the same structural components, but the curriculum involved a comprehensive schema-based approach to solving word problems. While both interventions stressed understanding of the concepts taught, the word-problem intervention placed a greater emphasis upon algebraic representations of problems posed.

Naturally an instruction-as-usual (or sort of, since RAs taught it) control was employed. Outcome variables included calculation, word problems, and pre-algebra problems, each divided into "distal" and "proximal" scores.

So how did this one come out? The authors said it best: "in terms of the specificity of effects of calculation and word problem instruction, results were in line with our hypotheses. Intervention improved performance in the targeted domain but not the other domain" (p. 1002). All of which is a more learned way of saying that students learned more of what they were taught and less of what they were taught less of what they weren't.

SUMMARY

This concludes our consideration of the eleven purposefully selected experiments conducted by Dr. Lynn Fuchs and her able team. And it is important to reiterate that these studies represent only a small sample of her experimental record, and experiments themselves constitute a minority of her other contributions which included curriculum development, the championing of sensible instructional/testing strategies, and even dabbling in brain-imaging efforts related to learning (e.g., Davis et al. 2009; Han et al. 2013).

However, the purpose of this little foray into the experimental work of an exemplary educational scientist was neither to celebrate her accomplishments nor criticize them. Rather it was designed to provide a case study of the potential for an individual educational researcher's decades-long efforts in this discipline to improve the utility and meaningful science of education.

But despite the expenditure of all those millions of dollars, it isn't apparent that the science of education has been advanced three inches if *its goal really is to improve classroom instruction*. Of course if the goal of the science is to repetitiously demonstrate that children will learn more if more (and more relevant) instruction is delivered to them then perhaps the money was well spent—especially for a science that appears to revel in demonstrations of the *obvious*.

Now, of course, no single individual can be held responsible for the lack of movement of any entire science, but does anyone reading thus far feel that perhaps, just perhaps, there may be something systemically wrong with that *science*? And that perhaps, just perhaps, the thought question proposed at the beginning of the book may not be so absurd after all?

Chapter 7

Research Genre #12: Recent, Well-Designed, Genre-Crossing Research Considered Important Enough to Be Reported in the Media

The *What Works Clearinghouse* (WWC) represents the US Department of Education's attempt to translate educational research findings into something actually useful to the schooling process. While the present author's attempts to accomplish a similar objective weren't exactly awe-inspiring based upon a review of the previous eleven research genres, this search would be incomplete without taking at least a cursory examination of some of the WWC's efforts.

Among other tasks, the WWC farms out the review of thousands of individual experiments accompanied by an assessment of their methodological quality. These relatively stringent methodological standards basically reduce to three operationally defined and totally defensible categories:

1. Meets WWC Group Design Standards without Reservations,
2. Meets WWC Group Design Standards with Reservations, or
3. Does Not Meet WWC Group Design Standards.

The experiments themselves appear to go back a little over two decades and as of October 2016, there were reputably 8,631 reviews of individual studies (mostly RCTs) of which 572 (6.6 percent) met the WWC's design standards without reservations. Two strategies were consequently employed by the present author to ascertain the degree to which these studies suggested any additionally directions (other than those mentioned in the previous chapters) that might improve the usefulness of the science.

The first strategy involved drawing a quasi-random sample of experiments from the 572 intervention studies judged to have met the WWC's standards "without reservations" (which basically entails randomization to groups, low attrition, and a lack of obvious confounding factors). However, after reviewing several dozen of these studies, their triviality was so overwhelming that this approach made the proverbial search for a needle in a haystack pale in comparison. (In other words, nothing useful was found, although this could of course be due to sampling error.)

The second strategy involved an executive decision to consider only those intervention studies that the WWC had designated as (a) meeting their standard without reservations *plus* (b) having garnered a degree of media attention. These experiments (forty in all) were designated by the WWC as single study "quick reviews" as of late 2015 and the present author downloaded all for the abovementioned purposes. (This turned out to be fortunate timing, since a few months later the WWC's website was drastically changed and these quick reviews were no longer readily identifiable as such—at least according to a response to a helpline query from the present author.)

This strategy of selecting examples of competent, contemporary educational experiments that garnered at least some media coverage would appear to be ideal for our purposes here. After all, what better criteria exist than well designed, relatively recent educational interventions that were judged as potentially important to the *public*? Or asked another way, wouldn't the public be more interested in practicality and the potential for improving the educational process than education professors or contractual employees?

SINGLE STUDY "QUICK REVIEWS"

Rather than attempt to discuss and summarize all forty of this disparate medley of studies, an attempt has been made to categorize them as defensibly as possible by experimental intent and then briefly discuss and abstract those that appear to represent lines of work that could result in increased student learning. The remainder will simply be listed and cited in the reference list. (Entering the information therein into a bowser will normally pull up the WWC abstract and/or the full study report.)

ONLINE AND DIGITALLY ASSISTED INSTRUCTION

In this book's companion volume, a case will be made that digital (or at least some form of technologically enhanced) instruction will basically constitute the future of instruction. In anticipation of that argument, the following four studies provide a sampling of some of the work already done in this area and perhaps a hint of how the medium could be expanded.

All four of these studies involved technologically enhanced instructional products and all four produced increased learning, access to instruction, or both. That they did not all rigorously control time, the curriculum, or the degree of correspondence between the test and the curriculum does not necessarily reduce their potential importance.

[1] *Digital algebra instruction* (Barrow, Markman, and Rouse 2009). High-school and middle-school classrooms randomly assigned (*random assignment was used in almost all of these studies so if it's not mentioned, it should be assumed unless an alternative assignment procedure is specified*) to use the commercial digital *I CAN Learn*® algebra instructional program (administered in the schools' computer labs) learned more than students taught in the traditional math curriculum taught in a regular classroom.

[2] *Access to digital algebra in rural middle school* (Heppen et al. 2012). This study employed four hundred students in sixty-eight rural middle schools randomly assigned to receive a stand-alone online algebra course or regular instruction. The students enrolled in the online course scored higher on an algebra exam than students enrolled in schools that did not offer a course exclusively dedicated to algebra (some algebra tended to be taught in the latter's traditional math classrooms). Instruction was provided by online course software that involved an "interactive electronic textbook focused on direct instruction and guided practice, practice problem sets with automated feedback, and quizzes and exams that offer immediate scores." Trained online tutors and in school proctors were also provided.

[3] *Digital rates and proportions instruction* (Roschelle et al. 2007). Students digitally taught rates and proportions learned more about the topic than those taught a "conventional unit" therein. (Neither time nor the curriculum appeared to be controlled.)

[4] *Reading textbooks, one involving a digitally supported curriculum, comparisons* (James-Burdumy et al. 2009). Four supplementary reading-comprehension curricula were compared to control. No differences were observed between the four curricula during the first year although the digitally supported curriculum (*ReadAbout*) was found to increase comprehension during the second year.

EXPERIMENTS ADDRESSING ACCESS
TO NONDIGITAL INSTRUCTION

Experiments addressing access to instruction via digital modalities were illustrated in the first section. However, any intervention that provides access to instruction not otherwise available, digital or otherwise, addresses an important need in education. Four exemplary studies involving access to additional relevant instruction all produced positive learning results and deserve expansion. One [5: *Free books for summer reading* (Allington et al. 2010)] involved distributing books for summer reading to economically disadvantaged first- and second-grade students. Students randomly assigned to receive these free books scored higher on reading tests than their controls after three years in the program. Why this inexpensive form of extra instruction couldn't be universally available to children, at least in impoverished school districts, is a complete mystery.

Two more important efforts involved the use of volunteer tutors [6: *Experience Corps Evaluation* (Morrow-Howell et al. 2009)] and [7: *Volunteer Tutors* (Jacob, Armstrong, and Willard 2015)], and one (discussed in detail in chapter 5) involved an impressive charter school effort in Harlem [8: *Harlem Charter School Evaluation* (Dobbie and Fryer 2009)] in which massive doses of extra instruction (much of it involving tutoring) produced (according to the authors) differential math and reading gains capable of wiping out the black–white achievement gap. (Perhaps the latter should be taken with a grain of salt, but the achievement gains were quite impressive.)

A fifth [9: *Head Start Mentoring* (Bierman et al. 2008)] involved increased access to instruction, which (as always) produced learning, but it can be described as potentially important only because it involved teaching *Head Start* students literacy, language development, and psychosocial skills. A similar Head Start study [10: *Number Games in Head Start* (Ramani and Siegler 2008)] compared playing games involving numbers versus colors and found that numeration skills were improved. And professionals wonder why large multicenter Head Start evaluations have often produced disappointing results! These two latter studies aren't mentioned here on their own merits. Rather they suggest that the entire Head Start program should be revamped under new leadership to administer more intensive instruction supported by tutoring.

FINANCIAL INCENTIVES

We've known for millennia that paying people is a good way to get them to do what we want, so on one level the results emanating from these studies are rather obvious. But education is the science of the obvious after all, so we shouldn't dismiss an obvious intervention that produces salutary educational outcomes out of hand. At least if said intervention isn't part of routine practice.

The first study [11: *Financial Incentives in a Four-City, Four-Conditions Study* (Fryer 2010)] in this category involved a four-city study, each with a different incentive for different genres of behavior. The only intervention of the four involving increased instructional time was (hardly coincidentally) also the only intervention that produced positive academic results. In this study, children were paid $2 per book for reading up to twenty books. (They were administered a brief quiz after reading each book to ensure that they actually had read it).

The next three studies all produced salutary results. One involved a much-debated policy topic (renewable scholarships up to $7,500 to attend private school) [12: *Private School Vouchers* (Wolf et al. 2010)], which produced no reading or math achievement effects but a significant high-school graduation rate even though many participants did not renew their scholarships. The second study awarded financial incentives for low-income adults newly enrolled in two community colleges [13: *Financial Incentives for Low-Income Parents Attending Community College* (Richburg-Hayes et al. 2009)] and resulted in their being more likely to reenroll the next year and to take more course work.

The third study [14: *CUNY's Comprehensive Accelerated Study in Associate Programs Initiative* (Scrivener et al. 2015)] described an impressive community-college program (ASAP) initiated by the City University of New York. The ASAP intervention was comprised of an extensive support system that included, among other things, tuition waver and free tutoring services. The randomly assigned ASAP students (in comparison to students receiving the system's usual services) accumulated significantly more college-level credits and were more likely to both attain a college degree or transfer to a four-year college (25 percent versus 17 percent) during the three-year study period (at an additional cost of $14,000 per student).

Only one [15: *Cash Awards to Low-Income Families* (Riccio, Dechausay, and Greenberg 2010)] of the four studies employing financially related incentives produced disappointing results. Not coincidentally, it was the only study that incentivized noninstructional behaviors.

STUDIES FUNDED BY NONTRADITIONAL SOURCES (H&R BLOCK AND THE NATIONAL GUARD)

Since one of the puposes of this book's companion volume is to explore infrastructure options for improving out science, any competently designed, nondemented educational research funded by outside sources should be welcomed. Two of our forty studies fit these conditions.

The first [16: *H&R Block FALSA Preparation* (Bettinger et al. 2009)] involved clients from 156 H&R Block tax-preparation offices randomly assigning clients to (a) receive help in completing the relatively time-consuming FALSA application, (b) provide information on it only, or (c) a no-treatment control. The clients receiving actual help were more likely to submit the application and both interventions increased the total amount of federal grants received for financially independent adults.

The second study [17: *National Guard Mentoring* (Bloom, Gardenhire-Crooks, and Mandsager 2009)] involved an experimental National Guard mentoring high-school dropouts randomly assigned to receive an intervention involving a twenty-two-week quasi-military residential phase followed by a year of mentoring services. Significant differences were obtained favoring the intervention over control that included an impressive 46 percent versus 10 percent rate of obtaining a high-school diploma or GED within nine months as well as increasing the rates of employment and enrollment in college.

DIFFICULT TO CLASSIFY BUT WORTHWHILE TOPICS TO EXPLORE FURTHER

Brief abstracts are presented for the following studies because of their potential importance and/or interesting approaches:

[18] *Science Terms vs. Everyday Language* (Brown and Ryoo 2008). Presently, textbooks are by far the most widely used instructional products. Head-to-head learning comparisons between them are difficult because some may be more closely keyed to testing content than others. However, this study resides in the product developmental realm and therefore potentially informs the writing of any textbook that does not already introduce important scientific concepts using nontechnical language.

Here, students were randomly assigned to be taught a lesson on photosynthesis (a) which began by explaining scientific concepts in everyday language and the content was only later linked with scientific language versus (b) the same content introduced using scientific language from the onset. The first group scored higher immediately after the lesson on their understanding of photosynthesis using scientific language.

[19] *Reading Instruction for Bilingual Children* (Slavin et al. 2010). Teaching bilingual children to read in English rather than teaching them in Spanish first before transitioning them to reading in English resulted in significantly better English reading and language skills than students in the transitional group. The effect gradually decreased over time until there were no significant differences by the fourth grade.

Comment: This is an important study, especially given the number of bilingual children entering our public schools. The positive result for learning to read in the language in which students will ultimately be taught is predicted by our working hypothesis, which in no way decreases its importance. The fact that the advantage of the English first intervention dissipated over time is not an indictment of the intervention but a common finding emanating from the inability of the schools to capitalize on prior learning.

[20] *Recitation as a Study Skill* (Karpicke and Blunt 2011). This study is mentioned for two reasons only. First, the development of effective study

skills may not appear to be an example of an instructional product, but is—just not a product anyone can hold or print out.

Second, the study is an example of the repetitiveness of current educational research and its brief institutional memory. The intervention, which involved retrieval practice was shown to be superior to three other conditions, had been shown to be an effective study skill at least twice over the past *century* for brief, content dense prose: once in 1917 by A. I. Gates and once in a quasi-replication by DelGiorno, Jenkins, and Bausell (1974) in which instructional time was controlled.

Naturally, neither study was cited by the authors of the present study, perhaps because they weren't aware that our science went back so far. And while research into different study skills will undoubtedly continue into the future, the outcome variable should be the time students are willing to devote to a new procedure versus their usual study methods.

PROFESSIONAL DEVELOPMENT AND TEACHER CERTIFICATION

Professional development, teacher certification, and teacher education have traditionally had no effect upon student achievement and there are no exceptions or surprises here. And while we didn't need these particular negative studies to inform us that none of these variables affect student achievement, perhaps the first study [21] possesses some importance. Not because it demonstrates anything new, but because it constitutes a well-designed experiment that once again demonstrates that teachers trained in schools of education do not elicit more learning from those not so trained.

[21] *Impacts of the Teach for America Scale-Up Evaluation* (Clark et al. 2015). Approximately thirty-seven hundred prekindergarten through fifth-grade students were randomly assigned within schools to either a Teach for America (TFA) instructor with one to two years of experience or a teacher with a different accreditation (the majority being trained in schools of education). No differences were observed in student achievement between the two groups, although one subgroup analysis (which should always be interpreted cautiously) indicated a statistical significant effect for reading favoring TFA teachers in the lower grades.

[22] *The Effects of National Board Certification* (Cantrell et al. 2008). Experienced Los Angeles teachers who applied for National Board for Professional Teaching Standards (NBPTS) certification and those who did not were paired and then classrooms of students were randomly assigned to each pair. Naturally no difference in student test scores accrued.

[23] *Professional Development for High-School Teachers* (Allen et al. 2011). Training plus coaching (*My Teaching Partner-Secondary Program*

[MTP-S]) was compared to treatment as usual. No difference was obtained during the first year but a positive post hoc effect was found for the former during the second. However, the WWC did not consider this latter finding to have met its standards due to differential attrition in the intervention group.

[24] *Alternative Routes to Teacher Certification and Student Achievement* (Constantine et al. 2009). Students within schools and grade levels were randomly assigned to one of two paired types of teachers: those who chose an alternative-certification versus a traditional-certification route. No statistically significant differences with respect to standardized test scores of students were observed between the two types of teachers. Same question: *Again, why doesn't anyone know this?*

[25] *Professional Development for Early Reading Teachers* (Garet et. al. 2008). Ninety schools were randomly assigned to teacher development involving (a) eight days of training based upon an experimental curriculum, (b) the same training plus coaching (one-to-one weekly support throughout the school year), and (c) business as usual. The teacher training (with or without the instructional coaches) did not increase their students' reading test scores. Why should it?

[26] *Professional Development for Middle-School Mathematics Teachers* (Garet et al. 2011). A relatively intense professional development intervention including instruction to teachers on the mathematical content as well as methods of explaining rational numbers and correcting misconceptions was compared to no such training. No significant differences with respect to student achievement were observed. Maybe we should bag teacher development as a research topic?

[27] *Comprehensive Teacher Mentoring/Support for Beginning Teachers* (Glazerman et al. 2008). The intervention was comprised of (a) weekly meetings with trained mentors, (b) classroom observation with feedback, and (c) monthly professional-development meetings. The control group was (you guessed it), business as usual. No effects were observed for teacher retention (the purpose of the intervention). As is often the case, positive results were observed in later years but this was probably due to attrition and would not have met the WWC standards.

THE REMAINDER OF THE "QUICK REVIEWS"

The remainder of the forty studies contained in the WWC's 2015 database of well-designed "Quick Reviews" that managed to garner some media attention are difficult to categorize. Many also don't appear to be particularly relevant to our purpose here for the reasons briefly mentioned below.

[28–29] *Math Textbook Evaluations* (Agodini et al. 2009; 2010). Textbook evaluations would appear to be an important research activity, but different texts (like standardized tests) inevitably give different emphases to different topics—hence the match between the two can produce artifactual differences favoring the text with the closest matches with a particular test (or tests).

[30] *DOE's Student Mentoring Program* (Bernstein et al. 2009). The student mentoring here did not involve instruction, hence it had no effect upon learning. Perhaps the Department of Education is misnamed? Or at least should be careful what interventions it lends its name to.

[31] *Example of a Scale-Up Experiment* (Campuzano et al. 2009). This boondoggle was reviewed (rather unfavorably) in chapter 4.

[32] *Freshman-Year Email Reminders Regarding FAFSA Renewal among Other Things* (Castleman and Page 2014). Reminding students of upcoming deadlines is a fine institutional policy, but most people wouldn't consider it *science*. It was also only tangentially (i.e., via a subgroup analysis) effective.

[33] *Writing Essays Has Wondrous Effects* (Cohen et al. 2009). Middle-school students were randomly assigned to write from three to five essays for approximately fifteen minutes each during the school year on either (a) personal value topics or on (b) neutral subjects. In a subgroup analysis, African American students writing on personal values obtained grade-point averages a quarter of a point higher than African American students writing on neutral topics. This one definitely needs replication if anyone considers it important enough to do so.

[34] *Supplementary Literacy Instruction* (Corrin et al. 2009). Ninth-grade students reading from two to five years below grade level were randomly assigned to receive two types of additional literacy instruction involving eleven hours per month of extra instruction versus none. The supplemental literacy classes led to statistically significant increases in student test scores for reading comprehension. Obvious, do you think?

[35] *Providing Exercise to Overweight Children* (Davis et al. 2011). This study produced positive results with respect to math achievement (the effect on weight loss wasn't mentioned) and should be replicated because the etiology of the effect is not exactly clear. Although this would be an important effect if it did replicate.

[36] *22 Site Charter School Evaluation* (Gleason et al. 2010). This is basically a meta-analysis (Genre #6) showing that some schools producing positive results and some negative ones. And as usual with this genre, too many have been conducted and too few have informed us about anything useful. Certainly freedom of choice mandates that charter schools, public schools, private schools, religious schools, home schools, and any other *category* of schools should be allowed to exist, but the choice of a *category* of schooling

does not impact learning irrespective of students' home learning environments. Only the provision of large doses of extra, more relevant instruction does that, as illustrated by the Harlem charter school evaluation above [8] and discussed in chapter 5.

[37] *Rewards Based upon Personal vs. Group Performance* (Hurley, Allen, and Boykin 2009). In a small-scale study that should be replicated before being taken too seriously, fourth- and fifth-grade African American students performed better in groups in which the rewards were group based rather than groups rewarded on an individual basis.

[38] *Middle-School Abstinence Education* (Jemmott III, Jemmott, and Fong 2010). Middle schools serving African American communities were randomly assigned to receive (a) an abstinence-only education program (designed to increase knowledge about sexually transmitted diseases, the health benefits of abstinence, and to teach skills designed to help students resist pressure to engage in sex) versus (b) a general health-promotion program. Two years later the abstinence educational group reported less sexual activity than the control.

[39] *Pizza Slices vs. Mathematical Symbols* (Kaminski, Sloutsky, and Heckler 2008). Undergraduates were taught mathematical concepts using (a) abstract symbols versus (b) three groups taught by using different numbers of concrete examples (e.g., slices of pizza, measuring cups filled with liquid). Abstract symbols were best, which may be why symbols are used in higher-level mathematics instead of pizza slices. Or perhaps it was just an accident of history that mathematical symbols were invented before pizza.

[40] *Students Taught a Topic Will Learn More Than Students Taught Something Else* (Penuel et al. 2009). Low-income children were randomly assigned to receive either a technology-enhanced literacy curriculum or a control group consisting of science instruction. Incredibly, the two groups were tested only on literacy. Hopefully by now you can guess the results of this one.

SUMMARY

It is difficult to imagine a more disparate group of experiments than the forty preceding studies. Most were well designed and employed adequate sample sizes. Only a few were *completely* inane and a few others would need to be replicated before anyone gets too excited about their somewhat surprising results. As a gestalt, these studies hopefully provided a useful snapshot of the type of modern educational research that manages to garner a certain measure of societal interest in a discipline far removed from the cultural mainstream.

However, the primary reasons for this exercise was, as always, to see if any of these studies informed our original thought question (since all of these studies were conducted in this century). While a forty-study sample can't possibly be representative of the tens of thousands of studies conducted during this time period, they were not designed to be representative. Instead, they were chosen because they were, after all, selected by both the WWC *and* the media presumably based upon their *potential* impact on the educational process. But from the perspective of this book's thought question, it is difficult to conceive how any (or the total group) could have possibly had any salutary impact upon public schools as a whole. Certainly some may have the potential to do so, but *potential* is a long trek from reality.

A second purpose of this chapter, however (perhaps more relevant to this book's companion volume than this one, which is more interested in clinical impact), was to ascertain which (if any) types of research might be useful for informing a meaningful science of education. In other words:

Do any of these areas of inquiry have potential for the science going forward?

And as a number of the comments accompanying these studies indicate, some may. First, almost any work designed to increase *access to instruction* or that employs digital instruction (the latter having the potential to both increase access as well as making instruction more *efficient*) is potentially important. Thus experiments [1–9 and 11–15] were all *potentially* useful.

Second, any work capable of increasing engagement (which in turn increases learning) is also pursuing and this was the crux of the financial incentive interventions in studies [11–15]. Financial incentives represent a powerful form of reinforcement, and the power of reinforcement to affect behavior has been recognized for several millennia before educational research was invented. And over half a century ago, it was successfully introduced as an adjunct to instruction and to facilitate engagement of special-education students in the form of tokens exchangeable for various rewards by Skinnerian adherents. But the financial incentives represented in these studies are a completely different animal.

And finally, the concept of research involving corporate interventions (e.g., the H&R Block [16] and the National Guard's effort [17]) taking place outside of the school setting should be encouraged, since they do not involve the expenditure of public educational funds that could be used for direct instruction.

Where to Go and How We *Might* Be Able to Get There from Here

By this point, surely no one questions what the present author's response to the originally proposed thought question is. And for those who have forgotten, that question was:

> *If no educational research had been conducted during this century, would this have deleteriously impacted the American public schools?*

For the record, however, the present author's answer is an unqualified and emphatic "NO!"

Now, of course, this answer isn't particularly helpful since educational research will continue to be conducted into the distant future. And even if its funds are cut by the present administration, they will almost certainly be restored generously by a future one.

So perhaps a more relevant question might be:

> *If no educational research were to be conducted in the future, would anyone but college professors, assorted beltway bandits, and think tank denizens be any worse off?*

However, this is a very difficult question to answer by a devout mentee of the two greatest scientific philosophers of all time: William of Occam *and* Yogi of Bronx (the latter warning us that "prediction is difficult especially about the future"). So rather than offend anyone, this particular question won't be answered.

A more useful thought question (or at least its answering) might therefore be:

> *What kind of educational research* might *improve student learning (in or outside of American public schools) in the future?*

117

And that, Dear Reader, is the subject matter of this book's companion volume entitled *Creating a Useful Science of Education: Society's Most Important and Challenging Task.* There, specific proposals for different genres of research and specific studies within those genres are proposed which (a) readers are encouraged to conduct (with or without attribution) and (b) funders are encouraged to support in order to reform the science of education.

Not necessarily to make it less obvious, because education may well always hold the honor of being the most obvious of sciences. Rather to make it more useful, for that is its only reason for this science's existence.

An equally important issue, once that question has been answered, involves the infrastructural components necessary to conduct these proposed research programs. These too are delineated in this book's companion volume—including a "Big Science" project that might just jumpstart the proposed reform and its required infrastructure.

References

Aaronson, D., Barrow, L., and Sanders, W. (2007). Teacher and student achievement in the Chicago public high schools. *Journal of Labor Economics* 25:95–135.

Achilles, C. M., Nye, B. A., Zaharias, J. B., and Fulton, B. D. (1993). *The Lasting Benefits Study (LBS) in grades 4 and 5 (1990–1991): A legacy from Tennessee's four-year (K–3) class-size study (1985–1989), Project STAR.* Paper presented at the North Carolina Association for Research in Education. Greensboro, North Carolina, January 14, 1993.

Adams, M. J. (1994). *Beginning to read: Thinking and learning about print.* Cambridge, MA: MIT Press.

Agodini, R., Harris, B., Atkins-Burnett, S., Heaviside, S., Novak, T., and Murphy, R. (2009). *Achievement effects of four elementary school math curricula: Findings from first graders in 39 schools* (NCEE 2009–4052). Washington, DC: National Center for Education Evaluation and Regional Assistance, Institute of Education Sciences, US Department of Education.

Agodini, R., Harris, B., Thomas, M., Murphy, R., Gallagher, L., and Pendleton, A. (2010). *Achievement effects of four early elementary school math curricula: Findings for first and second graders* (NCEE 2011–4001). Washington, DC: National Center for Education Evaluation and Regional Assistance, Institute of Education Sciences, US Department of Education.

Allen, J., Pianta, R., Gregory, A., Mikami, A., and Lun, J. (2011). An interaction-based approach to enhancing secondary school instruction and student achievement. *Science* 333:1034–37.

Allington, R. L., McGill-Franzen, A., Camilli, G., Williams, L., Graff, J., Zeig, J., et al. (2010). *Addressing summer reading setback among economically disadvantaged elementary students.* Washington, DC: Office of Educational Research and Improvement, US Department of Education, Grant # R305T010692-02.

Amrein-Beardsley, A. (2008). Methodological concerns about the education value-added assessment. *Educational Researcher* 37:65–75.

Amrein-Beardsley, A., and Collins, C. (2012). The SAS education value-added assessment system (SAS® EVAAS®) in the Houston Independent School District

(HISD): Intended and unintended consequences. *Education Policy Analysis Archives* 20 (12). http://epaa.asu.edu/ojs/article/view/1096.

Atkinson, R. C., and Jackson, G. B. (Eds.). (1992). *Research and education reform.* Washington, DC: National Academy Press.

Barrow, L., Markman, L., and Rouse, C. E. (2009). Technology's edge: The educational benefits of computer-aided instruction. *American Economic Journal: Economic Policy* 1:52–74.

Bausell, R. B. (2015). *The Design and Conduct of Meaningful Experiments Involving Human Participants: 25 Scientific Principles.* New York: Oxford University Press.

———. (2010). *Too Simple to Fail: A Case for Educational Change.* New York: Oxford University Press.

Bausell, R. B., and Li, Y. F. (2002). *Power Analysis for Experimental Research: A Practical Guide for the Biological, Medical, and Social Sciences.* Cambridge: Cambridge University Press.

Bausell, R. B., Moody, W. B., and Walzl, R. N. (1973). A factorial study of tutoring versus classroom instruction. *American Education Research Journal* 10:591–97.

Berliner, D. C. (2002). Educational research: The hardest science of all. *Educational Researcher* 31 (8):18–20.

Bernstein, L., Dun Rappaport, C., Olsho, L., Hunt, D., and Levin, M. (2009). *Impact evaluation of the US Department of Education's Student Mentoring Program* (NCEE 2009–4047). Washington, DC: National Center for Education Evaluation and Regional Assistance, Institute of Education Sciences, US Department of Education.

Bettinger, E., Long, B., Oreopoulos, P., and Sanbonmatsu, L. (2009). *The role of simplification and information in college decisions: Results from the H&R Block FAFSA experiment* (NBER Working Paper No. 15361). Cambridge, MA: National Bureau of Economic Research.

Bierman, K. L., Domitrovich, C. E., Nix, R. L., Gest, S. D., Welsh, J. A., Greenberg, M. T., et al. (2008). Promoting academic and social-emotional school readiness: The Head Start *REDI* program. *Child Development* 79:1802–17.

Bloom, B. S. (1976). *Human Characteristics and School Learning.* New York: McGraw Hill.

Bloom, D., Gardenhire-Crooks, A., and Mandsager, C. (2009). *Reengaging high-school dropouts: Early results of the National Guard Youth ChalleNGe Program evaluation.* New York: MDRC.

Bloom, H. S., Hill, C. J., Black, A. B., and Lipsey, M. W. (2008). Performance trajectories and performance gaps as achievement effect-size benchmarks for educational interventions. *Journal of Research on Educational Effectiveness* 1:289–328.

Boggess, L. (2010). Tailoring new urban teachers for character. *American Educational Research Journal* 47:65–95.

Boring, E. G. (1923). Intelligence as the tests test it. *New Republic* 36:35–37.

Bracht, G. H. (1970). Experimental factors related to aptitude-by-treatment interactions. *Review of Educational Research* 40:627–45.

Brophy, J. (1986). Teacher influences on student achievement. *American Psychologist* 41:1069–77.

Brown, B. A., and Ryoo, K. (2008). Teaching science as a language: A "content-first" approach to science teaching. *Journal of Research in Science Teaching* 45:529–53.

Bugelski, B. R. (1962). Presentation time, total time, and mediation in paired-associate learning. *Journal of Experimental Psychology* 63:409–12.

Bus, A. G., van Ijzendoorn, M. H., and Pellegrini, A. D. (1995). Joint book reading makes for success in learning to read: A meta-analysis on intergenerational transmission of literacy. *Review of Educational Research* 65:1–21.

Campuzano, L., Dynarski, M., Agodini, R., and Rall, K. (2009). *Effectiveness of reading and mathematics software products: Findings from two student cohorts* (NCEE 2009–4041). Washington, DC: National Center for Education Evaluation and Regional Assistance, Institute of Education Sciences, US Department of Education.

Cantrell, S., Fullerton, J., Kane, T. J., and Staiger, D. O. (2008). *National board certification and teacher effectiveness: Evidence from a random assignment experiment* (NBER Working Paper 14608). Cambridge, MA: National Bureau of Economic Research.

Castleman, B. L., and Page, L. C. (2014). *Freshman year financial aid nudges: An experiment to increase FAFSA renewal and college persistence.* EdPolicyWorks Working Paper Series No. 29. Charlottesville, VA: EdPolicyWorks.

Chubbuck, S. M. (2004). Whiteness enacted, whiteness disrupted: The complexity of personal congruence. *American Educational Research Journal* 41:301–33.

Cilesiz, S. (2009). Educational computer use in leisure contexts: A phenomenological study of adolescents' experiences at internet cafés. *American Educational Research Journal* 46:232–74.

Clark, M. A., Isenberg, E., Liu, A. Y., Makowsky, L., and Zukiewicz, M. (2015). *Impacts of the Teach for America Investing in Innovation Scale-Up.* Princeton, NJ: Mathematica Policy Research.

Cohen, G. L., Garcia, J., Purdie-Vaughns, V., Apfel, N., and Brzustoski, P. (2009). Recursive processes in self-affirmation: Intervening to close the minority achievement gap. *Science* 324:400–403.

Cohen, J. (1988). *Statistical power analysis for the behavioral sciences* (2nd Edition). Hillsdale, NJ: Lawrence Erlbaum.

Cohen, P. A., Kulik, J. A., and Kulik, C. L. C. (1982). Educational outcomes of tutoring: A meta-analysis of findings. *American Educational Research Journal* 19:237–48.

Coleman, J. S., et al. (1966). *Equality of educational opportunity.* Washington, DC: US Department of Health, Education and Welfare.

Constantine, J., Player, D., Silva, T., Hallgren, K., Grider, M., and Deke, J. (2009). *An evaluation of teachers trained through different routes to certification: Final report* (NCEE 2009-4043). Washington, DC: National Center for Education Evaluation and Regional Assistance, Institute of Education Sciences, US Department of Education.

Cooley, W. W., and Leinhardt, G. (1980). The Instructional Dimensions Study. *Educational Evaluation and Policy Analysis* 2:7–25.

Cooper, E. H., and Pantle, A. J. (1967). The total-time hypothesis in verbal learning. *Psychological Bulletin* 68:221–34.

Corrin, W., Somers, M.-A., Kemple, J., Nelson, E., and Sepanik, S. (2009). *The Enhanced Reading Opportunities study: Findings from the second year of implementation* (NCEE 2009–4036). Washington, DC: National Center for Education Evaluation and Regional Assistance, Institute of Education Sciences, US Department of Education.

Craig, C. J. (2006). Why is dissemination so difficult? The nature of teacher knowledge and the spread of curriculum reform. *American Educational Research Journal* 43:257–93.

Cronbach, L. J. (1957). The two disciplines of scientific psychology. *American Psychologist* 12:671–84.

———. (1975). Beyond the two disciplines of scientific psychology. *American Psychologist* 30:116–27.

Curran, P. J. (2009). The seemingly quixotic pursuit of a cumulative psychological science: introduction to the special issue. *Psychological Methods* 14:77–80.

Davis, C. L., Tomporowski, P. D., McDowell, J. E., et al. (2011). Exercise improves executive function and achievement and alters brain activation in overweight children: A randomized, controlled trial. *Health Psychology* 30:91–98.

Davis, N., Cannistraci, C. J., Rogers, B. P., Gatenby, J. C., Fuchs, L. S., Anderson, A. W., Gore, J. C. (2009). The neural correlates of calculation ability in children. *Magnetic Resonance Imaging*, 27: 1187–1197.

DelGiorno, W., Jenkins, J. R., and Bausell, R. B. (1974). Effects of recitation on the acquisition of prose. *Journal of Education Research* 67:293–95.

Deno, S. L. (1985). Curriculum-based measurement: The emerging alternative. *Exceptional Children* 52:219–32.

Elizabeth, T., Anderson, T. L. R., Snow, E. H., and Selman, R. L. (2012). Academic discussions: An analysis of instructional discourse and an argument for an integrative assessment framework. *American Educational Research Journal* 49:1214–50.

Ennemoser, M., and Schneider, W. (2007). Relations of television viewing and reading: Findings from a 4-year longitudinal study. *Journal of Educational Psychology* 99:349–68.

Enright, K. A. (2011). Language and literacy for a new mainstream. *American Educational Research Journal* 48:80–118.

Finn, J. D., Gerber, S. B., and Boyd-Zaharias, J. (2005). Small classes in the early grades, academic achievement, and graduating from high school. *Journal of Educational Psychology* 97:214–23.

Fisher, C. W., Berliner, D. C., Filby, N. N., et al. (1980). Teaching behaviours, academic learning time, and student achievement: An overview. In A. Lieberman and C. Denham (Eds.). *Time to Learn: A Review of the Beginning Teacher Evaluation Study.* Washington, DC: National Institute of Education, Dept. of Health, Education and Welfare.

Fryer, R. G. (2010). *Financial incentives and student achievement: Evidence from randomized trials* (NBER Working Paper 15898). Cambridge, MA: National Bureau of Economic Research.

Fuchs, D., Fuchs, L. S., Mathes, P. G., and Simmons, D. C. (1997). Peer-assisted learning strategies: Making classrooms more responsive to diversity. *American Educational Research Journal* 34:174–206.

Fuchs, L. S., Compton, D. L., Fuchs, D., et al. (2005). The prevention, identification, and cognitive determinants of math difficulty. *Journal of Educational Psychology* 97:493–513.

Fuchs, L. S., Fuchs, D., Bentz, J., Phillips, N. B., and Hamlett, C. L. (1994). The nature of student interactions during peer tutoring with and without training and experience. *American Educational Research Journal* 31:75–103.

Fuchs, L. S., Fuchs, D., and Craddock, C., et al. (2008). Effects of small-group tutoring with and without validated classroom instruction on at-risk students' math problem solving: Are two tiers of prevention better than one? *Journal of Educational Psychology* 100:491–509.

Fuchs, L., Fuchs, D., Hamlett, C., et al. (1997). Enhancing students' helping behavior during peer-mediated instruction with conceptual mathematical explanations. *Elementary School Journal* 97:223–49.

Fuchs, L. S., Fuchs, D., Hamlett, C. L., and Karns, K. (1998). High-achieving students' interactions and performance on complex mathematical tasks as a function of homogeneous and heterogeneous pairings. *American Educational Research Journal* 35:227–67.

Fuchs, L. S., Fuchs, D., and Karns, K. (2001). Enhancing kindergartners' development: Effects of peer-assisted learning strategies. *The Elementary School Journal* 101:495–510.

Fuchs, L. S., Fuchs, D., Phillips, N. B., et al. (1995). Acquisition and transfer effects of classwide peer-assisted learning strategies in mathematics for students with varying learning histories. *School Psychology Review* 24:604–20.

Fuchs, L. S., Fuchs, D., and Yazdian, L., et al. (2002). Enhancing first-grade children's mathematical development with peer-assisted learning strategies. *School Psychology Review* 31:569–83.

Fuchs, L. S., Geary, D. C., Compton, D. L., et al. (2013). Effects of first-grade number knowledge tutoring with contrasting forms of practice. *Journal of Educational Psychology* 105:58–77.

Fuchs, L. S, Powell, S. R, Cirino, P. T., et al. (2014a). Does calculation or word-problem instruction provide a stronger route to prealgebraic knowledge? *Journal of Educational Psychology* 106:990–1006.

Fuchs, L. S., Powell, S. R., Seethaler, P. H., et al. (2009). Remediating number combinations and word problem deficits among students with mathematics difficulties: A randomized control trial. *Journal of Educational Psychology* 101:561–76.

Fuchs, L. S., Schumacher, R. F., Sterba, S. K., et al. (2014b). Does working memory moderate the effects of fraction intervention? An aptitude-treatment interaction. *Journal of Educational Psychology* 106:499–514.

Gardner, H. (1983). *Frames of Mind: The Theory of Multiple Intelligences.* New York: Basic Books.

Garet, M. S., Cronen, S., Eaton, M., et al. (2008). *The impact of two professional development interventions on early reading instruction and achievement* (NCEE 2008–4030). Washington, DC: National Center for Education Evaluation and Regional Assistance, Institute of Education Sciences, US Department of Education.

Garet, M., Wayne, A., Stancavage, F., et al. (2011). *Middle-school mathematics professional development impact study: Findings after the second year of implementation* (NCEE 2011–4024). Washington, DC: National Center for Education Evaluation and Regional Assistance, Institute of Education Sciences, US Department of Education.

Gates, A. I. (1917). Recitation as a factor in memorization. *Archives of Psychology* 40. https://archive.org/stream/recitationasfact00gaterich/recitationasfact00gaterich_djvu.txt

Glass, G. V. (1976). Primary, secondary, and meta-analysis of research. *Educational Researcher* 5:3–8.

Glass, G. V., and Smith, M. L. (1979). Meta-analysis of research on class size and achievement. *Educational Evaluation and Policy Analysis* 1:2–16.

Glass, G. V., Cahen, L. S., Smith, M. L., and Filby, N. N. (1982). *School Class Size: Research and Policy*. Beverly Hills, CA: Sage.

Glazerman, S., Dolfin, S., Bleeker, M., Johnson, A., Isenberg, E., Lugo-Gil, J., Grider, M., and Britton, E. (2008). *Impacts of comprehensive teacher induction: Results from the first year of a randomized controlled study* (NCEE 2009–4034). Washington, DC: National Center for Education Evaluation and Regional Assistance, Institute of Education Sciences, US Department of Education.

Gleason, P., Clark, M., Tuttle, C. C., and Dwoyer, E. (2010). *The evaluation of charter school impacts: Final report.* Washington, DC: National Center for Educational Evaluation and Regional Assistance, Institute of Education Sciences, US Department of Education.

Gould, S. J. (1981). *The Mismeasure of Man.* New York: Norton.

Graesser, A. C., and Person, N. K. (1994). Question asking during tutoring. *American Educational Research Journal* 31:104–37.

Han, Z., Davis, D., Fuchs, L., Anderson, A., Gore, J. C., Dawant, B. M. (2013). Relation between brain architecture and mathematical ability in children: A DBM study. *Magnetic Resonance Imaging* 31:1645–56.

Hand, V. M. (2010). The co-construction of opposition in a low-track mathematics classroom. *American Educational Research Journal* 47:97–132.

Hanushek, E. A. (2011). The economic value of higher teacher quality. *Economics of Education Review* 30:466–79.

Hart, B., and Risley, T. R. (1995). *Meaningful differences in the everyday experience of young American children.* Baltimore, MD: Paul H. Brookes.

Hartley, S. S. (1977). *Meta-analysis of the effects of individually paced instruction in mathematics.* Unpublished doctoral dissertation, University of Colorado, Boulder, CO. *Dissertation Abstracts International*, 1977, *38(1-A), 4003.* (University Microfilms No. 77-29,926).

Hattie, J. (2009). *Visible learning: A synthesis of over 800 meta-analyses relating to achievement.* London: Routledge.

Heppen, J. B., Walters, K., Clements, M., Faria, A., Tobey, C., Sorensen, N., and Culp, K. (2012). *Access to Algebra I: The effects of online mathematics for grade 8 students* (NCEE 2012–4021). Washington, DC: National Center for Education Evaluation and Regional Assistance, Institute of Education Sciences, US Department of Education.

Hill, H. C., Rowan, B., and Ball, D. L. (2005). Effects of teachers' mathematical knowledge for teaching on student achievement. *American Educational Research Journal* 42:371–406.

Hurley, E. A., Allen, B. A., and Boykin, A. W. (2009). Culture and the interaction of student ethnicity with reward structure in group learning. *Cognition and Instruction* 27:121–46.

Jacob, R. T., Armstrong, C., and Willard, J. A. (2015). *Mobilizing volunteer tutors to improve student literacy: Implementation, impacts, and costs of the Reading Partners program*. New York: MDRC.

James-Burdumy, S., Mansfield, W., Deke, J., et al. (2009). *Effectiveness of selected supplemental reading comprehension interventions: Impacts on a first cohort of fifth-grade students* (NCEE 2009–4032). Washington, DC: National Center for Education Evaluation and Regional Assistance, Institute of Education Sciences, US Department of Education.

Jemmott J. B. III, Jemmott, L. S., and Fong G. T. (February 2010). Efficacy of a theory-based abstinence-only intervention over 24 Months: A randomized controlled trial with young adolescents. *Archives of Pediatrics and Adolescent Medicine* 164:152–59.

Jenkins, J. R., Dale, P. S., Mills, P. E., et al. (2006). How special education preschool graduates finish: status at 19 years of age. *American Educational Research Journal* 43:737–81.

Jeynes, W. H. (2002). The challenge of controlling for SES in social science and education research. *Educational Psychology Review* 14:205–21.

Johnson, P. O., and Neyman, J. (1936). Tests of certain linear hypotheses and their application to some educational problems. *Statistical Research Memoirs* 1:57–93.

Kaestle, C. F. (1993). The awful reputation of education research. *Educational Researcher* 22:23–26.

Kaminski, J. A., Sloutsky, V. M., and Heckler, A. F. (2008). The advantage of abstract examples in learning math. *Science* 320:454–55.

Karpicke, J. D., and Blunt, J. R. (2011). Retrieval practice produces more learning than elaborative studying with concept mapping. *Science* 331:772–75.

Kelly, S., and Price, H. (2011). The correlates of tracking policy: Opportunity hoarding, status competition, or a technical-functional explanation? *American Educational Research Journal* 48:560–85.

Kemp, L. C. D. (1955). Environmental and other characteristics determining attainment in primary schools. *British Journal of Educational Psychology* 25:67–77.

Kulik, J. A., Bangert, R. L., and Williams, G. W. (1983). Effects of computer-based teaching on secondary school students. *Journal of Educational Psychology* 75:19–26.

Lagemann, E. C. (2000). *An elusive science: The troubling history of educational research*. Chicago: University of Chicago Press.

Lieberman, A. and Denham, C. (Eds.). (1980). *Time to learn: A review of the beginning teacher evaluation study*. Washington, DC: National Institute of Education, Dept. of Health, Education and Welfare.

Lipsey, M. W., Puzio, K., Yun, C., et al. (2012). *Translating the statistical representation of the effects of education interventions into more readily interpretable forms*. (NCSER 2013–3000). Washington, DC: National Center for Special Education Research, Institute of Education Sciences, US Department of Education. http://ies.ed.gov/ncser/

Lipsey, M. W., and Wilson, D. B. (1993). Educational and behavioral treatment: Confirmation from meta-analysis. *American Psychologist* 48:1181–209.

Mathes, P. G., and Fuchs, L. S. (1994). The efficacy of peer tutoring in reading for students with mild disabilities: A best-evidence synthesis. *School Psychology Review* 23:59–80.

Morrow-Howell, N., Jonson-Reid, M., McCrary, S., Lee, et al. (2009). *Evaluation of Experience Corps: Student reading outcomes*. St. Louis: Washington University, George Warren Brown School of Social Work, Center for Social Development.

Moody, W. B., and Bausell, R. B. (1971). *The effect of teacher experience on student achievement, transfer, and retention.* Paper presented at the 1971 meeting of the American Educational Research Association at New York.

Moody, W. B., Bausell, R. B., and Jenkins, J. R. (1973). The effect of class size on the learning of mathematics: A parametric study with fourth-grade students. *Journal of Research in Mathematics Education* 4:170–76.

Nisbett, R. E. (2009). *Intelligence and how to get it: Why schools and cultures count.* New York: Norton.

Nye, B., Konstantopoulos, S., and Hedges, L. V. (2004). How large are teacher effects? *Educational Evaluation and Policy Analysis* 26:237–57.

O'Connor, R. E., and Jenkins, J. R. (1996). Cooperative learning as an inclusion strategy: A closer look. *Exceptionality: A Special Education Journal* 6:29–51.

Open Science Collaboration. (2015). Estimating the reproducibility of psychological science. *Science* 349, aac4716 (1–7).

Park, C. C. (2011). Young children making sense of racial and ethnic differences: A sociocultural approach. *American Educational Research Journal* 48:387–420.

Penuel, W. R., Pasnik, S., Bates, L., Townsend, E., Gallagher, L. P., Llorente, C., and Hupert, N. (2009). *Pre-school teachers can use a media-rich curriculum to prepare low-income children for school success: Results of a randomized controlled trial.* New York and Menlo Park, CA: Education Development Center, Inc. and SRI International.

Peterson, P. L. (1998). Why do educational research? Rethinking our roles and identities, our texts and contexts. *Educational Researcher* 27:4–10.

Polman, J. L., and Miller, D. (2010). Trajectories of identification among African American youth in a science outreach apprenticeship. *American Educational Research Journal* 47:879–918.

Popham, W. J. (1997). The moth and the flame: Student learning as a criterion of instructional competence. In J. Millman (Ed.), *Grading Teachers, Trading Schools: Is Student Achievement a Valid Evaluation Measure?* Thousand Oaks, CA: Corwin Press.

———. (1971). Performance tests of teaching proficiency: Rationale, development, and validation. *American Educational Research Journal* 8:105–17.

Powell, M. (1980). The Beginning Teacher Evaluation Study: A brief history of a major research project. In A. Lieberman and C. Denham (Eds.). *Time to learn: A review of the Beginning Teacher Evaluation Study.* Washington, DC: National Institute of Education, Dept. of Health, Education and Welfare.

Ramani, G. B., and Siegler, R. S. (2008). Promoting broad and stable improvements in low-income children's numerical knowledge through playing number board games. *Child Development* 79:375–94.

Riccio, J., Dechausay, N., Greenberg, D., Miller, C., Rucks, Z., and Verma, N. (2010). *Toward reduced poverty across generations: Early findings from New York City's conditional cash transfer program.* New York: MDRC.

Richburg-Hayes, L., Brock, T., LeBlanc, A., Paxson, C., Rouse, C. E., and Barrow, L. (2009). *Rewarding persistence: Effects of a performance-based scholarship program for low-income parents.* New York: MDRC.

Roschelle, J., Tatar, D., Schectman, N., Hegedus, S., Hopkins, B., Knudsen, J., and Stroter, A. (2007). *Scaling up SimCalc project: Can a technology enhanced curriculum improve student learning of important mathematics?* (Technical Report 01). Menlo Park, CA: SRI International.

Rosenshine, B. (1970). The stability of teacher effects upon student achievement. *Review of Educational Research* 40:647–62.

Rothstein, J. (2010). Teacher quality in educational production: Tracking, decay, and student achievement. *The Quarterly Journal of Economics* 125:175–214.

Sanders, W., and Rivers, J. (1996). *Cumulative and residual effects of teachers on future student academic achievement.* Knoxville, TN: University of Tennessee Value-Added Research and Assessment Center.

Sanders, W. L., Wright, S. P., and Langevin, W. E. (2009). The performance of highly effective teachers in different school environments. In *Performance incentives: Their growing impact on American K–12 education*, M. G. Springer (Ed.), Washington, DC: Brookings Institution Press.

Scrivener, S., Weiss, M. J., Ratledge, A., et al. (2015). *Doubling graduation rates: Three-year effects of CUNY's Accelerated Study in Associate Programs (ASAP) for developmental education students.* New York: MDRC.

Senechal, M., and LeFevre, J. (2002). Parental involvement in the development of children's reading skill: A five-year longitudinal study. *Child Development* 73:445–60.

Silverman, S. K. (2010). What is diversity? An inquiry into preservice teacher beliefs. *American Educational Research Journal* 47:292–329.

Slavin, R. E., Madden, N., Calderon, M., Chamberlain, A., and Hennessy, M. (2010). *Reading and language outcomes of a five-year randomized evaluation of transitional bilingual education.* Baltimore, MD: Johns Hopkins University.

Sroufe, G. E. (1997). Improving the "awful reputation" of educational research. *Educational Researcher* 5:26–28.

Steenbergen-Hu, S., and Cooper, H. (2013). A meta-analysis of the effectiveness of intelligent tutoring systems on K–12 students' mathematical learning. *Journal of Educational Psychology* 105:970–87.

Thorndike, Edward L. (1911). *Animal intelligence: Experimental studies.* New York: Macmillan.

Watson, J. D., and Crick, F. (1953). A structure for deoxyribose nucleic acid. *Nature* 171:737–38.

Wolf, P., Gutmann, B., Puma, M., Kisida, B., Rizzo, L., Eissa, N., and Carr, M. (2010). *Evaluation of the DC Opportunity Scholarship Program: Final report* (NCEE

2010–4018). Washington, DC: National Center for Education Evaluation and Regional Assistance, Institute of Education Sciences, US Department of Education.

Word, E., Johnston, J., Bain, H. P., et al. (1994). *Student/Teacher Achievement Ratio (STAR): Tennessee's K–3 class size study. Final summary report 1985–1990.* Nashville: Tennessee Department of Education. http://d64.e2services.net/class/STARsummary.pdf

Ylimaki, R. M., and Brunner, C. C. (2011). Power and collaboration-consensus/conflict in curriculum leadership. *American Educational Research Journal* 48:1258–85.

Index

About the Author

R. Barker Bausell, PhD, is a research methodologist, biostatistician, educational researcher, and author of this book's companion volume: *Creating a Useful Science of Education: Society's Most Important and Challenging Task*. He has written twelve other books including *The Conduct and Design of Meaningful Experiments Involving Human Participants*, *Too Simple to Fail: A Case for Educational Change*, and *Snake Oil Science* (all published by Oxford University Press), and *Power Analysis for Experimental Research* (Cambridge University Press). He was the first educational researcher to demonstrate that tutoring could produce significantly more learning than both classroom and small-group instruction within a thirty-minute time period when student and teacher differences, time, and the curriculum were rigorously controlled.

He was also the founding editor and editor-in-chief for thirty-three years of the premiere, refereed health-evaluation journal *Evaluation & the Health Professions* and served as professor and research director in two University of Maryland academic departments during that time period. He has worked with a number of other organizations including serving as (a) the director of the Prevention Research Center of Rodale Press (which publishes *Prevention Magazine*), (b) the methodological and statistical consultant for *Discover Magazine,* (c) a senior scientist for the Delmarva Foundation for Medical Care (which evaluates Medicare and Medicaid programs), and (d) as a research/statistical consultant for several other institutions.